Praise for *The Dog's Table*

"It turns out that my dog Tucker's purpose is . . . treats! I was raised by a father who cooked gourmet meals for the dogs and ordered pizza for the kids. As for me, I love to cook for the whole family, so I will treasure this book's recipes—they are safe and delicious for any four-legged family members. For all the love they give us, giving them nutritious whole foods feels like the right thing to do. Tucker especially loved his Eggs Benedog!"

—W. Bruce Cameron, #1 *New York Times* bestselling author of *A Dog's Purpose*

"*The Dog's Table* is a fun, science-backed resource for anyone looking to improve their dog's nutrition and health through real food. Joelle Jay and R. A. Young have done an exceptional job combining evidence-based insights with practical, easy-to-follow recipes that support canine health at every life stage.

I appreciate how this book challenges outdated pet food norms and instead promotes whole-food nutrition, a key factor in both human and canine health. The authors skillfully debunk myths surrounding dog diets while providing a balanced, accessible approach to home-prepared meals.

The Dog's Table is not just a cookbook, it's a movement toward better nutrition, better health, and ultimately, better lives for our four-legged companions."

—Matt Kaeberlein, PhD, biologist and founder and codirector of the Dog Aging Project

"As a veterinarian committed to helping dogs live longer, I'm thrilled to see *The Dog's Table* boldly challenge the outdated norms of pet feeding. This book is clear, practical and deeply researched—reminding us that dogs deserve more than ultra-processed convenience. The philosophy aligns powerfully with what I advocate every day: fresh, whole foods, nutrient diversity, and feeding without fear. It's a much-needed resource that empowers dog parents with both knowledge and joy."

—Dr. Will Maginness, veterinarian

"As an integrative nutritionist, I'm impressed by *The Dog's Table* for its evidence-based approach to canine nutrition, emphasizing whole, home-cooked meals that prioritize gut health and optimal ingredient quality. The book's practical recipes and focus on balanced diets across life stages make it an invaluable resource for pet owners seeking to nourish their dogs with wholesome, scientifically grounded food. I can't wait to utilize it for my doggos!"

—Courtney Swan, MS, creator of the *Realfoodology* podcast

"Unbelievable read! From somebody who has tested recipes for dogs over a hundred times, this book is so informative for dog parents who are searching for homemade recipes. A comprehensive, yet simple and fun way to understand home cooking for your dog. Home cooking is such an easy way to ensure your dog is getting the best quality food for their health. Which in itself is worth every penny . . . you won't regret it!"

—Charlie from Cherry Hoggs, dog psychologist and trainer

THE
DOG'S TABLE

**120+ Easy Real-Food Recipes for Happier,
Healthier Pups—from Eggs Benedog to Seafood Pawella**

JOELLE JAY and R. A. YOUNG

BenBella

BenBella Books, Inc.
Dallas, TX

BENBELLA

BenBella Books, Inc.
8080 N. Central Expressway
Suite 1700
Dallas, TX 75206
benbellabooks.com
Send feedback to feedback@benbellabooks.com

BenBella is a federally registered trademark.

Printed in the United States of America
10 9 8 7 6 5 4

The Library of Congress Cataloging-in-Publication Data is available upon request.
ISBN 9781637747766 (hardcover)
ISBN 9781637747773 (electronic)

Editing by Leah Wilson and Claire Schulz
Copyediting by Jennifer Brett Greenstein
Proofreading by Becky Maines and Sarah Vostok
Indexing by Debra Bowman
Text design and composition by Kit Sweeney
Cover design by Joelle Jay and Brigid Pearson
Cover and interior photography by Joelle Jay
Lifestyle photography on pages vi, viii, 2, 10, 12, 14, 16, and 23 by Anna Lueck
Photograph on page 14 (inset) by Roger Clemens

Special discounts for bulk sales are available. Please contact bulkorders@benbellabooks.com.

To our best friends,
past, present, and future.
We hope that this book
brings you better lives.

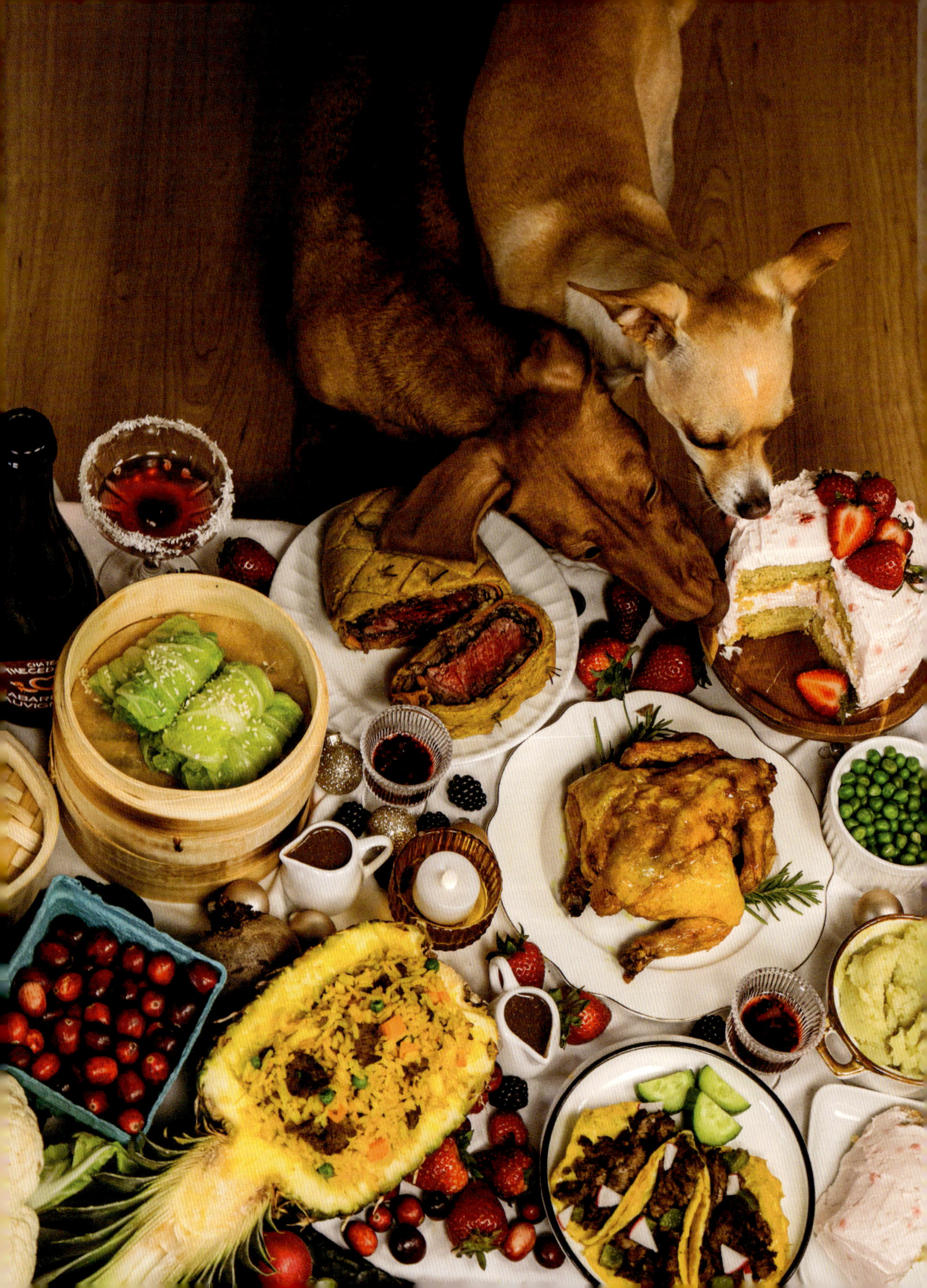

Contents

Introduction

Dogs experience food, too.

Imagine you were transported to a world where your nose was 100,000 times more sensitive than it is now. This superpower would allow you to smell in 3D. Food and beverages would have deep, complex aromas that evolved over seconds and minutes. You would be able to smell exactly how the food was cooked. You would notice minute details about your drinks, like the makeup of the soil where a wine was grown. You would even be able to taste the diet of the animals you ate.

Your sensitivities would also be amplified. Just as people wear sunglasses to protect their eyes from harsh light, you might seek products to block out offensive smells, too. Foods like garlic and heavy spices that seep through the skin might be banned in some places.

This superpower actually exists in our world—not for people, of course, but for dogs. Most people don't realize just how extraordinarily sensitive dogs' noses are. Dogs' senses of smell are so acute that they can track people and prey across miles, smelling the subtle changes of the scent molecules over long distances. There are even dogs that are specially trained to smell cancer. Dogs can smell concentrations as low as one part per trillion (ppt). To put this in perspective, 1 ppt is approximately 1 drop in 20 Olympic-sized swimming pools.[1]

The reason dogs can smell so acutely is that their brains are designed for it. While they have 10 times the number of olfactory cells in their noses as humans do, the brain region devoted to processing smells is also about 40 times larger than ours, relative to brain size. However, dogs aren't as smart as humans, so their awareness of these scents is lower. Also, they are less prone to disgust, so they are not as averse to bad smells as we are.

Instead of unpleasantness, like people may experience, this sensitivity gives dogs great pleasure. They *love* to smell. When most dogs go outside, their immediate reaction is to sniff everything and everyone around them.

Since smell, taste, and appetite are closely linked, we are quite sure that dogs' appreciation of delicious smells and their sensory experience of food are very real. Every time there is something good cooking in the kitchen, our dogs, Cedric and Edith, use smell to distinguish if it's our food or theirs.

Dogs that don't eat real food probably wonder why it's only people who get to eat the good stuff. When they whine and beg for our food, we see this as purely bad behavior. We might momentarily feel guilty for giving them dog food when we get various tasty meals, but then we tell ourselves that dog food is what's best for them, and that they can't taste the difference anyway. The reality is that dogs probably enjoy food as much as or more than people do. There's even research suggesting that smell and taste do help dogs enjoy food.[2] Why not let them have the *good stuff* every day?

Why Feed Real Food?

Many of us are used to feeding our dogs dry kibble from bags or wet dog food from cans, unaware that home-cooked dog food is really easy to make. Although we like to have fun cooking for our pups (as our punny recipe titles will attest), cooking for dogs isn't silly, and it's not spoiling them. Home-cooked

food is far better than highly processed commercial dog food and more nutritious than even the freshest premade food you can buy. There are several reasons for this. The first is enhanced nutrient absorption and bioavailability. Micronutrients like vitamins and minerals from whole foods are generally more bioavailable (meaning the body can use them more easily) than synthetic forms. For example, nutrients like vitamins A, E, and folate are all more active in their natural forms. Real food has multiple health benefits—from complex carbohydrates and fiber that benefit the gut, to antioxidants, phytonutrients, and enzymes that support cellular health—that make it so much better than kibble (more on that later).

The second reason is safety. Synthetic vitamins can often be helpful supplements to whole foods, but today's dog food is made nutritionally complete mostly through synthetic additives rather than naturally nutrient-dense ingredients. Toxicity is an issue with some synthetic vitamins. For example, vitamin A, folic acid (the synthetic form of folate), and vitamin D are more toxic than their natural counterparts. These synthetic versions tend to build up in tissue, which can lead to toxicity and organ damage. (They are also easy to overdo, as evidenced by multiple vitamin D–related recalls.)

And, finally, another benefit of practicing your culinary skills on dog food is that it will

almost certainly be enjoyed. Unless the food is burned or undercooked, you can feed your pups whatever you create, no matter how it turns out. Not only will they eat it, but they will likely be very appreciative of your efforts—unlike some of your human family members.

Through reading this book and trying your hand at the daily recipes, you will learn the components of a balanced canine diet made with real whole foods. As you venture into our doggy dining experiences, you will start to stretch your culinary skills. No matter your cooking ability, all of these recipes will make your dogs healthier and happier!

Why Listen to Us?

We are Joelle and R. A., the creators behind Thecedlife, the dog foodie social media channel. Our two pups, Cedric and Edith, enjoy gourmet meals fit for the finest three-paw restaurants. We post recipes and write a weekly newsletter called *Precious Kitchen*, sharing in-depth research on canine health, diet, and wellness. Also, we launched a line of all-natural dog food mixes and spices from our website www.preciouscreatures.co to help people make the freshest, most nutritious food for their dogs at home.

We take our commitment to you and your dogs seriously and have analyzed thousands of research papers on dog nutrition and health. We've consulted the leading researchers on dog (and human) longevity. We've looked into anecdotes, myths, and stories about toxic foods and uncovered low-quality research papers used as original sources. (More on that in "What Not to Feed Your Dog," page 21.) In addition, we researched the nutrition curriculum in veterinary schools and did deep dives on the Association of American Feed Control Officials (AAFCO) requirements. We even audited the leading dog food formulation software, and because we found so many mistakes, we built our own.

It's hard to believe that this all started with a video of Cedric eating pancakes on TikTok.

People liked it so much we started making and serving more elaborate meals. You might have seen one of our videos. Our presentation of Bark Wellington, Chicken Adogbo, and Spawghetti and Meatballs helped earn us over 300 million views and about 2 million followers in the first 18 months.

We don't know exactly why our videos are popular, but we have a few guesses. First, people just love dogs. Also, something about the way dogs eat is really funny and endearing. Perhaps it's because dogs do the things that people wish they could, but don't because of social niceties. Or maybe it's because people can identify with the feelings they see in the dogs.

Whatever the reason, something about our content has struck a chord—and, beyond just funny videos, many of our followers also want better food for their own dogs but don't know where or how to begin. People are coming to realize that commercial dog food is made for convenience, and not for dog health. This convenience comes at a cost, just like human fast food does. More and more people want to change the way they feed their dogs but are held back by fear and a lifetime of false information. We know because we once felt the same.

We aren't veterinarians or nutritionists. We don't have any certifications, nor are we seeking any. But that's the whole point. Do you have to consult a nutritionist before you eat a meal or feed your child? (We'll spare you the issues with nutritional epidemiology.) Do you have to be a doctor to write a cookbook? (Never mind that doctors don't study much nutrition in medical school.) Most reasonable adults don't bat an eye when a kid eats a cupcake—but when a dog eats anything other than dog food, people go nuts. How did this happen? Why are we turning to vets and for-profit companies to govern how we feed our dogs?

You might think that vets, as animal health experts, are uniquely qualified to say what a dog should be eating. Most vets are going to tell you it's wrong to feed your dog real food, but **veterinarians are not required to study dog nutrition**. It's not that vets don't care or want ill health for your dog. It's just that providing detailed nutritional advice is not what they are trained to do. They treat disease, prescribe medication, and perform lifesaving surgeries.

On top of their demanding workload, vets are trained to care for multiple disparate species. The average vet isn't a specialist in dog nutrition, or nutrition for any animal. The simplest and safest thing for vets to do is recommend kibble. Kibble is endorsed by the governing bodies in the industry, and vets don't have any incentive to challenge that. Most veterinary clinics also sell dog food, which is a big conflict of interest. (This is not so strange, considering that the largest manufacturer of dog food in the United States is also the largest employer of vets.) So, despite their best intentions, when it comes to food for dogs, vets often instill irrational fear and perpetuate old myths.

In reality, the concept of "dog food" is actually something someone made up about 100 years ago. Food is food, and real, whole foods are beneficial to us all. If you're someone who prioritizes your health, loves to cook, and loves your dog, you'll likely agree. As with human health, dog health starts with good, wholesome food.

In this book we share our experience, research, and simple meals to provide your dog the tastiest and healthiest food. We also devote a large portion to culinary experiences for you and your pups, family, and friends to enjoy together.

Joelle, dog chef and content creator of Thecedlife

I was set on feeding Cedric kibble when I brought him home in November 2022. Years before, I had tried to make homemade meals for my childhood dogs. Although I had an inkling that real food was the right path, the lack of user-friendly resources, my self-doubt, and a huge mess in the kitchen had me scrapping the whole idea. I decided not to try again for Cedric because it felt too complicated and risky.

At 25, after a stressful year of packing up my life in Shanghai and moving back to the United States, I wanted life with my new pup to be simple. Things don't usually go as planned, and Cedric proved to be no exception. He came home with a fluffy bed, a big bag of kibble, and a course of antibiotics. At just eight weeks old, he was being treated for a stomach bug his whole litter had contracted. His little life started out with an upset tummy. The kibble, because of his sensitive gut, resulted in tar-like poops and slimy vomit.

Already, my hopes to keep his diet simple were fading. He couldn't keep any food down. I was scared. I didn't want to "risk his life" by feeding him anything other than *vet-approved* food.

My partner, R. A., suggested that we give Cedric an egg. I went straight to Google to soothe my anxieties. I knew dogs could have eggs, but I couldn't let go of the irrational worry. "Can dogs have eggs?" "Can puppies have eggs?" "At what age can dogs have eggs?" I triple-checked. The online consensus was mostly yes, speckled with just enough warnings of allergies, potential diarrhea, and salmonella poisoning to keep me uneasy. *Only feed in moderation alongside a regular diet of dog food*, the articles all agreed.

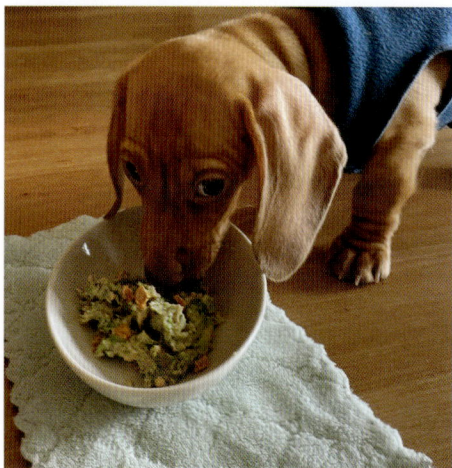

So we boiled an egg. "We have to make sure it's really cooked," I cautioned, even though I often eat runny eggs. (Sometimes the things we believe go against logic.) Of course, Cedric was delighted by the egg, and so was I, watching him happily wolf it down. Every bite of that boiled egg was life-changing for him, and ultimately for me.

Still reluctant to throw it out, I put the kibble away—but that kibble was never to be touched again. Even so, for months I still clung to the idea that Cedric needed dog products *of some kind* to stay healthy. Kibble alternatives, supplements, and treats filled up our shelves. After letting most of them go to waste, I finally realized what I was buying into—a false sense of security.

I needed to see "for dogs," "nutritionally complete," and other marketing claims to feel safe. The truth is that most manufacturers do the bare minimum to meet nutritional guidelines. They combine fillers and preservatives, using high heat and pressure to mold the food into convenient nuggets that last a long time on the shelf. Interestingly, if you look at the ingredient lists on dog food products, you'll see a range of ingredients derived from real foods—the same ingredients for which we often get criticism for serving to the dogs in our cooking videos.

Why does it only become "dog food" when it's overly processed, packaged, and labeled? Is it not ideal to feed those ingredients directly, in their freshest forms?

How would I feed my dog in a world where these products didn't exist?

These questions helped me let go of the validation the package labels gave me. By the time Edith joined us a year later, Cedric was doing well on real food and my confidence had grown. I cooked for Edith on her first day home without hesitation.

Thecedlife first began when I started a social media account for Cedric as a fun experiment, not expecting much. The views took off on a video of Cedric eating one of his homemade meals: a fancy stack of pancakes that drew lots of interest as well

thecedlife · 2023-6-23
Brunch eating sounds #nomusic
#brunch #doglife #dogsoftiktok... more

88.5K

880

4,742

on the cutting edge of human longevity science, an avid reader, researcher, and a great cook, too. Behind the scenes, he's analyzing paper after paper on dog nutrition, balancing our recipes, and managing the business. He's also Cedric and Edith's beloved dog dad.

R. A., lead researcher and formulator

I didn't actually want to get Cedric at first. We had just set up in the Pacific Northwest, after living in Asia for a long time, and I wasn't sure that we were going to stay. Also, because of family and work, I was planning to travel between the two places. What if we wanted to move? It would make things so much harder. But Joelle insisted that we get Cedric, and you all know what happened next.

For as long as I can remember, I've been skeptical of dog food. Years ago, I started feeding my family dog Oscar a raw carnivore diet. It was hard because sometimes he would throw up, and something about the diet just didn't feel right to me. I started to cook fresh food for him and his companion, Rocky. Both long-haired dachshunds, Oscar, like Cedric, was a brownish-red color and Rocky was black and tan. At the time, I wasn't deep into the research like I am now, but my gut feeling was that dry, processed food probably wasn't good for them. Yet even so, as I got older and busier, I ended up feeding them kibble. It was fast and cheap, but ultimately it was a mistake.

Later in life, Oscar suffered from bad tooth decay and poor health. In just a couple of years, he went from a spry older dog to an incontinent mess. All his teeth had to be removed. He lost his hearing first, and shortly afterward he lost his eyesight. It seemed like he was suffering, and he had to be put to sleep. Rocky, though several years younger, was on the same trajectory and started a decline at around 13 years old. At the time he was eating kibble with homemade food toppers, and just like Oscar, he eventually had many of his teeth removed. He was in

as criticism. Many were concerned it was hurting him.

I realized a lot of people were also confused about what dogs could eat, and something sparked. From there, our dog-friendly meals grew even more elaborate, and that's how Thecedlife transformed into the "gourmet" dog food page it is today. Fueled by so much misinformation, our theme quickly turned into a mission. Now, we are creating the resources that I wish I had back when I first attempted to feed my childhood dogs better.

Though you don't see him in our videos, R. A. has been building this platform with me all along. When I first needed to start balancing Cedric's daily food, I couldn't figure out how to do it. A couple of days and Excel sheets later, R. A. built us a nutrition calculator that was more accurate than the leading paid software. His approach to life is to challenge the norm. He's an experimenter intense pain. He would wince and whine, suffering from recurrent mouth infections.

I decided to switch Rocky to an exclusively whole-food homemade diet. Immediately, he started to perk up again. Within a few months, he was running around and the mouth infections improved. I knew that there was a link between food and health, but how quickly things changed was a surprise. This helped solidify my conclusion that chronic disease is mostly related to our food.

I've had a lot of experience with chronic diseases as they have been a part of my family for generations. My grandparents all had chronic diseases—diabetes, heart disease, hypertension, Graves' disease, and rheumatoid arthritis. My dad has suffered from type 2 diabetes since I was a kid. In his later years he experienced heart failure and had open-heart surgery and open-back surgery. My mom passed away when I was 10 after a grueling battle with cancer. I grew up believing I would suffer the same fate. I lived and worked hard, knowing that I could go at any moment.

Then, in 2017 I was diagnosed with severe sleep apnea. Although I was young, worked out regularly, and stayed in decent shape, I had bad breathing problems when I slept. If I didn't fix it, my chances of heart disease and sudden death would increase as I got older. It was not a quick death that scared me, but rather agonizing slow suffering that I wanted to avoid.

According to doctors, the only effective treatment was a continuous positive air pressure (CPAP) machine. I was skeptical, so I embarked on a journey to heal without one. This journey of self-healing led me down a path of biology and longevity science. I read study after study and digested as many books as possible on the topic. It seems obvious now, but at the time I didn't realize how much our habits affect our health. Not just the things we drink and eat, but also our

sleep, exercise, and even our relationships determine how well we age. According to numerous studies, the estimated contribution of genetics to health and longevity is only about 25 percent.[3] The vast majority of the factors that determine how well and how long we live are up to us. The prevailing evidence suggests that this is true for all animals, including dogs.

Knowing all this, Joelle and I were still inclined to feed Cedric kibble. The influence of pet food manufacturers is so strong that we ignored our own research into food quality and health. In many ways, the intestinal infection that Cedric had as a puppy was a gift. It helped us break free from our dependence on dry dog food.

After the reception of Thecedlife's videos, I really dug into the research on dog health and nutrition to make sure that "human food" wasn't harming Cedric. Also, I didn't want to lead anyone else to hurt their dogs. What I learned through reading thousands of papers was shocking and actually made me really sad. I had let my guard down as I got busier, just trusting that kibble was okay. Now, years later, I am convinced that kibble led to more suffering for Oscar, and I will never feed any animal this kind of food again.

While kibble may be a good tool when convenience is a priority (like when feeding hundreds of dogs in a shelter), it's no substitute for the real thing. The result of dogs eating processed foods is that they are now the unhealthiest that they have ever been. According to studies, more than 60 percent of adult dogs are obese or overweight.[4] The incidence of periodontal disease is now as high as 87 percent.[5] Rates of cancer in dogs are growing, along with obesity.[6]

All of this has us convinced that real food for dogs is the way to go. You can share the gifts of better health, more variety, and more enrichment for your dog in the form of real food—and you can rest assured they will still get everything they need. Read on to see why.

Dog Nutrition Basics

The vast majority of dogs in the world eat just to live. The same was true of people throughout most of our history. We lived off the land and ate whatever we could find. Flavor, quality, and nutrition were afterthoughts because our main objective was survival. It wasn't until 10,000 years ago that agriculture began, leading to the abundance that we have today.

Though 10,000 years sounds like a long time, in terms of evolution, it's the blink of an eye. So, while our genes haven't changed much since the dawn of agriculture, the way we live—and eat—is drastically different. Yet our dogs are still stuck in the dark ages of food. While most of us eat for a combination of taste and nutrition, most dogs get the worst of both worlds. They're stuck eating tasteless balls of dough with no aroma or depth of flavor. The food they do get is made nutritionally complete with synthetic additives.

Emerging fresh dog food companies offer glimpses of what a better future could look like, but their fresh/frozen wet dog food is often reminiscent of slop, albeit only because most companies make it that way. People don't realize kibble is made according to **optimal manufacturing specifications** rather than what's best for dogs—see the FAQs, page 15, for more on this.

Who are we to say what's best for dogs? After all, we make silly videos with dog puns. Maybe Barkshuka is a bit over the top, and if you're not a fan, you probably think Dog Julio Pawquila is way too cheesy. Though the names may be silly, our commitment to scientific rigor is very serious. Regardless, we'll hold the puns in the next section, where we summarize our research covering thousands of studies and decades of research.

What Do Dogs Really Need?

Dogs are categorized as facultative carnivores, which means that they prefer to eat animals but can digest a variety of plants. Humans are considered omnivores. However, because we evolved together over 10,000 years or more, dog digestive systems are starting to resemble ours. For example, domestic dogs now have enzymes to digest complex carbohydrates that their wild cousins, the wolf and dingo, do

---

WHAT ARE ESSENTIAL NUTRIENTS?

Essential nutrients are those nutrients that an organism needs but can't make on its own. For example, people have to get certain amino acids (the building blocks of proteins) and vitamins (like vitamin C) from plants and animals that make them. When a nutrient is called *nonessential*, it doesn't mean we don't need it; in biology, this term simply means that the body can produce that nutrient on its own, so we don't need to consume it in our food to fulfill our minimum requirements. That said, there is a lot of literature detailing the benefits of getting more of those nonessential nutrients from food and the drawbacks of not getting enough.

not.[7] (Interestingly, according to researchers, genes that code for these enzymes are not uniform across all dog breeds. For example, the Siberian husky has fewer copies—just three to four of them—of a gene that codes for starch digestion. The saluki, an ancient breed originating from the Fertile Crescent, has 29 copies.[8])

We're not telling you all this because we expect you to become an expert on canine biology. We simply want to assure you that **your dog can get all the essential nutrients they need from a diet similar to yours, and the literature backs this up**.

Nutrient requirements for healthy dogs are pretty similar to humans' nutrient requirements with a few key differences. This is why we often reference human nutrition data in our research into dog health. There is a lot of overlap, especially on essential nutrients. Let's take a look at what your dog really needs.

Dogs Need Protein

We've all heard we need to eat protein. But what does it do for us?

Dogs, humans, and most other mammals prefer to use protein to do things in cells. The protein hemoglobin, for example, transports oxygen from our lungs to our cells. Protein's biological functions make it a crucial part of our diets.

Herbivores like cows can create protein from eating plants. (Technically it's the bacteria in their guts that produce most of the protein.) Omnivores and carnivores like humans and dogs need to get protein, particularly essential amino acids, from their foods. Amino acids are the building blocks of protein. After an animal or human eats protein, the body breaks it down into amino acids that can be recombined to make new proteins. Dogs and humans have similar essential amino acid needs, but dogs have slightly higher requirements for some specific amino acids. (For example, taurine is a nonessential amino acid for dogs, but

underconsumption of taurine can lead to dilated cardiomyopathy in some breeds.) There are ten amino acids that dogs can't make and nine that people can't make.

Just how *much* protein dogs need has been a subject of study—and debate—for decades. A 1966 study estimated the minimum daily protein requirements of dogs to be between 0.4 and 0.6 grams per kilogram of body weight.[9] For comparison, recommended protein intake for humans ranges from 0.8 grams per kilogram of body weight for sedentary adults to 2.0 grams per kilogram or more for athletes. So that recommendation for dogs is likely too low due to the limitations of measuring and understanding nitrogen balance at that time.

On the other hand, a 2020 study showed that high-protein diets (46 percent dry matter) in dogs increased metabolites associated with kidney disease and increased proteolytic bacteria (those that break down and live off protein) in stools.[10] The increase of metabolites doesn't mean that high protein intake *causes* kidney disease, but it does indicate increased strain. Also, the presence of bacteria that live off protein in stools means that dogs aren't digesting excess protein and instead excrete it, where it is consumed by these bacteria. For these reasons, we believe a very high protein diet is not optimal for most dogs, either.

This is why the **maintenance recipes in this book aim for 30–35 percent of the calories from protein**. Of course, it's okay to go higher or lower than this on occasion or regularly if your dog doesn't digest carbohydrates well. Variety and variance keep dogs' digestive systems adaptable. Protein requirements are easily met by common proteins like chicken, beef, pork, and salmon, as well as some less common options like venison and bison.

Dogs Need Fats

Fats are the main energy source for people and dogs because fat is the densest form

ARE SUNFLOWER SEEDS SAFE?

We use sunflower seeds in our recipes despite avoiding sunflower oil. Feeding a small amount of sunflower seeds (for their vitamin E) is very different from using sunflower oil for cooking. Modern seed oils are heavily processed. They are extracted with chemicals, then bleached at high heat and finally deodorized to remove unpleasant smells. Not only are seed oils too high in omega-6 fatty acids, high heat can alter their chemical state.

Our main cooking oils are light olive oil, butter, clarified butter (or ghee), coconut oil, and tallow, and we eat a lot of raw extra-virgin olive oil. Olive oil is high in the monounsaturated fat oleic acid, which is linked with lower inflammation and heart health. Light olive oil has roughly the same fatty acid composition as extra-virgin olive oil but has the plant matter removed. This means it's safer for low-temperature cooking. For high-temperature frying, we prefer to use clarified butter, tallow, or coconut oil because they are much more stable at high temperatures.

of energy. Every gram of fat has 9 calories while each gram of carbohydrate has only 4 calories. Studies show that dogs' preferred diet has 60 percent or more of the calories from fat.[11] **Our maintenance recipes aim for about 50 percent of the calories from fat.**

Fats are often stored in animals together with protein, so on a real-food diet, most of your dog's fat intake will come from meat. Like proteins, oils and fats are made up of different fatty acids. Dogs and people both require omega-3 and omega-6 fatty acids. Omega-6 is plentiful in the food supply; oils like safflower oil and corn oil, which are used in processed foods, contain up to 80 percent omega-6.

Omega-3s are much harder to get, especially DHA and EPA, the ones that dogs and people really need. These are most commonly obtained from seafood. The plant version of omega-3, ALA, doesn't convert well to EPA or DHA in either dogs or people.[12] You may have heard that flaxseeds or hemp seeds are a good source of omega-3s, but that's only partly true. In order to get just 1 gram of DHA from those exclusively plant sources, the average person would need to eat almost a pound of seeds. Omega-3s are particularly important for brain and nervous system function in animals. For example, DHA plays a critical role in the function

and structure of synapses, where neurons communicate with one another.[13]

A number of scientists are studying the ideal ratio of omega-6 to omega-3 in humans, but this research is still emerging, and it's even more unclear for dogs. Still, there is good evidence that a lower omega-6 to omega-3 ratio is better. One highly cited literature review puts the ancestral ratio of omega-6 to omega-3 for people at 1:1.[14] Modern Western diets have a ratio greater than 15:1 on average, and researchers propose that this promotes cancer, heart disease, and autoimmune diseases, while the opposite (a higher intake of omega-3) has suppressive effects.

Two separate studies on omega-6 to omega-3 ratios in dogs suggest that lower is also better. In one small study, scientists first fed dogs a diet with an omega-6 to omega-3 ratio of 25:1 and then switched half of the subjects to a diet with a 5:1 ratio.[15] The researchers concluded that a lower ratio had a positive effect on immune response. Another study examined the response to a similar diet change in atopic dogs (those prone to eczema and allergies) and found that nearly half were able to resolve their symptoms.[16]

Additionally, a small study found that feeding dogs exclusively sunflower oil (which is very high in omega-6) caused the pancreas to work harder compared to exclusively feeding olive oil.[17]

To lower our omega-6 to omega-3 ratio, we feed/eat lots of fish and supplement with high-quality fish or krill oil for both the pups and ourselves. Fish oil goes rancid far more easily than krill oil and is only about half as bioavailable. The main drawback of krill oil is that it's more expensive and less potent than fish oil. If you feed fish oil, you can review third-party tests for oxidation by-products on the brands you buy and you can store opened containers in the refrigerator.

Do Dogs Need Carbohydrates?

Technically, no, dogs don't require carbohydrates. But it's not as simple as that.

Plants, the main source of biological energy on the planet, make carbohydrates from the sun (the process is called photosynthesis). Nearly all terrestrial creatures rely on this fundamental energy source. (Cats appear to be a rare exception and prefer to use protein for energy.)

Even so, carbs often get blamed for the increasing levels of obesity in people and dogs. It's easy to think that carbs are evil, but it's the type and amount of carbohydrates that matter. Highly refined carbohydrates cause trouble. Because most commercial dog foods are 40 percent or more refined carbohydrates, the vast majority of vets are recommending diets that we believe to be far too high in carbohydrates. On the other hand, some nutritionists and vets recommend zero or near-zero carbohydrates, and we believe this approach to be misguided as well.

One of the claims of very low carb proponents is that dogs do not require carbohydrates and thus should not consume them. This logic is flawed. Humans also don't technically require dietary carbohydrates. But there are many foods that humans don't technically require but are beneficial, like fermented foods, green tea, and some nuts and seeds.

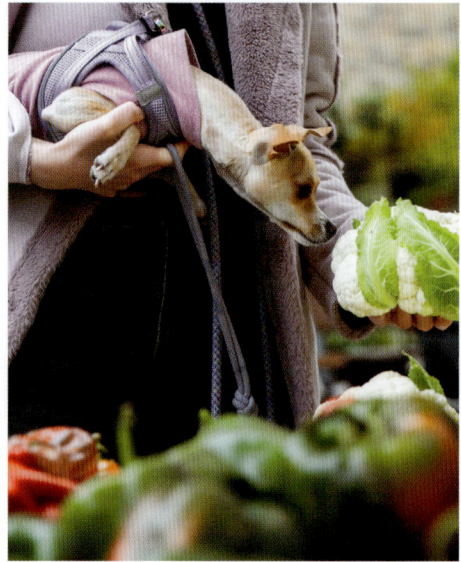

To get to the bottom of the carbohydrate debate, you have to consider carbs' structure and their function in the body. Carbohydrate, in its most basic form, is considered to be glucose, a sugar. When health care providers talk about blood sugar, they are referring to how much glucose is dissolved in the blood. Sugar is a basic nutrient in dogs and humans, as glucose is the preferred fuel of the brain. However, some cells, like red blood cells, can only run on glucose. This is one of the reasons there is sugar in the blood at all.

Sugar is so crucial for humans' and dogs' functioning that our bodies have a way to make sugars from proteins and fats: a process called gluconeogenesis. Even when a dog is starving, they will still have small amounts of blood glucose that is made through this process. Carbohydrates are considered to be nonessential nutrients simply because both dogs and people can make them.

However, making glucose via gluconeogenesis takes more energy than consuming it because it needs to be put together from smaller parts. For these reasons, we believe eating some dietary carbohydrates is good for both dogs and people. (Variety is also important, so sometimes we feed very low carbohydrate meals as well.)

When animals consume too much pure glucose or too many refined carbohydrates, the trouble begins. Pure glucose gets metabolized very quickly and spikes blood sugar. Frequent blood sugar spikes are harmful for several reasons:

1. High blood sugar stresses the endocrine system and causes the pancreas and kidneys to work harder.
2. Blood sugar spikes also result in blood sugar crashes, which may increase hunger and create a spike-crash cycle.
3. Increased blood sugar and increased insulin lead to weight gain, metabolic syndrome, and chronic disease.

Pure glucose is not readily available in nature. It is usually found in fruits or plants and typically makes up only a small portion of carbohydrates. To store glucose, plants connect the molecules into chains of increasing complexity. From complex carbohydrates to fibers and even cellulose, all of these structures are based on glucose molecules strung together.

The more complex the carbohydrate, the longer it takes to break down and turn into the glucose that raises blood sugar. Fiber, which is indigestible and usually accompanies sugar and starches in nature, also slows down digestion. This complexity allows a nice, slow, and even release of glucose into the bloodstream.

Carbohydrates in today's food supply, however, are often refined to increase purity and remove fiber; refined carbs are cheaper to transport for manufacturers and also more appealing to our animal brains. Breads, crackers, cookies, and pasta are made to be very calorically dense. Kibble, too, is typically made with refined carbohydrates and thus spikes your dog's blood sugar. This is probably the reason for exploding rates of obesity and subclinical pancreatitis in dogs.

Ultimately, the literature suggests that including plant matter and carbohydrates is beneficial for most dogs. In our experience, we also find that our dogs tend to do better on a diet that includes some complex carbs. Of course, there are exceptions. These exceptions tend to be due to genetics or when dogs are pushed to the extremes of physical performance. For example, several studies show that working dogs that require a constant level of aerobic output perform best on a near-zero-carbohydrate diet. Sled dogs, herding dogs, and working dogs are more active when fed these ultra-low-carbohydrate, high-protein diets.[18] Conversely, racing dogs fed similar diets, with high protein and high fat, are slower than when they are fed moderate-protein, moderate-fat diets with higher carbohydrates.[19]

Since most dogs are companion animals, the vast majority of our daily recipes will include up to 20 percent of the calories from carbohydrates. However, as mentioned previously, there are some breeds that are less able to digest carbs, and it's likely that the variance can exist on an individual level as well. Also, senior dogs tend to need less carbohydrates, so we include low-carb recipes in our athlete, senior, and weight-loss sections. Experimenting with the different recipes will help you find what works best for your pup.

We use the following sources of carbohydrates for our pups and ourselves:

- 🐾 Whole grains like quinoa (technically a seed), farro, rice (we love Haiga rice), steel cut, and rolled oats
- 🐾 Vegetables like sweet potatoes, carrots, beets, and squash
- 🐾 Fruits like berries, bananas, melons, and apples, usually as snacks

Dogs Need Micronutrients

Vitamins and minerals are essential nutrients that are needed in small amounts. Because there are many micronutrients, this section will highlight just the main differences between dogs' and people's needs. Also, we will discuss some harder-to-get micronutrients. The main differences in

2. For vitamin E, we use roasted, unsalted sunflower seeds or wheat germ. Wheat germ oil and sunflower oil are also high in vitamin E, though we don't typically use either.

3. We include calcium in our recipes by adding eggshells. The ratio of calcium to phosphorus isn't typically a concern unless too much calcium is added.

4. Zinc and copper are abundant in beef, venison, bison, and oysters, so we feature these foods.

5. Vitamin D is high in fatty fish like salmon and moderate in eggs, and these foods appear in many of our recipes.

6. Sea kelp (*Ascophyllum nodosum*) is the main source of iodine in our recipes.

If you keep in mind these six points, you can start to formulate your own dog food. It's really that simple.

vitamin and mineral needs between dogs and humans can be summarized as follows:

1. Unlike people, dogs can synthesize vitamin C and don't require it in their diets.

2. Dogs require vitamin D, while people can synthesize vitamin D through exposure to sunlight.

3. Dogs have higher requirements of vitamin A, some B vitamins, and vitamin E.

4. Dogs have higher requirements of some minerals like zinc, copper, and calcium, while also requiring a calcium to phosphorus ratio lower than 2:1.

5. Just like people, dogs need iodine, which can be difficult to get (that's why people use iodized salt—but in most instances, adding salt isn't ideal for dog food).

These requirements can be met with a few basic additions:

1. Adding a bit of organ meat like liver can make up for most of the vitamin B requirements. Beef liver is particularly nutrient dense and also contains zinc, copper, vitamin A, and many other vitamins and minerals.

A Quick Overview on "Balance"

One of the main objections to feeding homemade meals is that it's harder to ensure that the food is appropriately balanced. You may have heard that AAFCO or National Research Council (NRC) standards are important to follow, but you might not know why. Here's a quick primer.

All animals—including humans—need a balance of essential nutrients, often referred to as a balanced diet. However, because animals all evolved in competitive environments, we've also evolved to store important nutrients in our bodies. For this reason, animals thrive on balanced *diets*, but every *meal* does not need to be perfectly balanced.

For animal feed in America, AAFCO is the governing body. As noted earlier, this voluntary organization is made up of government officials who set the standards for nutritional profiles, ingredient definitions, product labels, and more for animal feeds. They do not regulate the pet food industry, but they set the standards to which feed manufacturers must adhere. The NRC, a US government organization, also publishes a set of guidelines for dog nutrition. However, because the NRC does not hold any regulatory authority, we focus our attention (and gripes) on AAFCO.

When pet foods are labeled "balanced" and "complete," this means that the food in the package meets the standards set by AAFCO. These standards cover more than 14 species, including poultry, cattle, and fish in addition to dogs and cats. Because they cover so many species, and also because every animal has individual differences, these guidelines are very broad. In some instances, they are incomplete; for example, AAFCO does not include guidelines for omega-3s EPA and DHA, which we covered earlier. They do not have recommendations for senior dogs, and the minimum protein requirement is 18 percent dry matter, while the minimum fat requirement is 5.5 percent for adult dogs. This means that dog food can legally be up to 70 percent carbohydrate, which, based on our research, is totally inappropriate.

Commercial dog food has to be fortified with all required nutrients because refined carbs are short on most vitamins and minerals. Also, for most modern dogs, it's the only thing they ever eat, day in and day out. The only time balanced meals would be necessary for people is if we also ate the same exact thing for every meal. If a person ate only cereal, for example, they would be severely malnourished as they would not be getting essential nutrients. The cereal would have to be fortified with the entire daily required intake to keep the body going in the long term. On the other hand, if someone eats a diet that includes different foods every day, they are probably covering their minimum nutrient requirements. If it's a colorful mix of whole foods—fruits, vegetables, meats, fish, fats, and grains— they're likely thriving. (There is research showing that as many as 50 percent of people are subclinically deficient in some nutrient, but that's a topic for another book.)

When dogs eat a varied diet, as people do, most of the concerns with balance no longer apply. There is both anecdotal and scientific evidence that this is true. The oldest dogs on record, like Bluey, Bramble, and Bobi, generally ate whole-food diets. These anecdotes are backed up by science. According to a study done by Waltham (owned by Mars, a global leader in kibble, no less), **dogs fed unbalanced home diets did not show any signs of deficiency.**[20] There could be multiple explanations for this. The first is that the nutrients in natural foods are more bioavailable than synthetic additives. The second is that current nutritional recommendations could be inaccurate. Lastly, it could just be that balance only matters if dogs are eating the same meal every day. It's probably a mix of all three.

However, we must acknowledge that just because the dogs in this study did not show *signs* of nutrient deficiencies doesn't mean that the dogs were not nutrient deficient. Dogs are highly adaptable and can remain healthy on diets severely deficient in essential nutrients for long periods of time. A simple diet of rice, ground beef, and carrots, fed over years, for example, would likely lead to deficiencies in several vitamins and minerals. Luckily, it doesn't take too many more ingredients to remedy that, and you'll find plenty of simple recipes that cover all the nutrients your dog needs in this book.

In short, we believe that variety is the best way to ensure that your pup has the nutrition and varied plant matter to support the ecosystem that lives in their belly. We also believe that a balanced overall diet is more important than having every meal balanced. Although our Balanced and Supermeal recipes are formulated to exceed AAFCO guidelines, we don't believe you need to worry about making *all* your dog's meals balanced, day in and day out.

As mentioned previously, we built a proprietary nutrition calculator so that we can ensure the accuracy of our formulations.

(There are plenty of nutrition calculators online, but we've found numerous mistakes in the most common ones.) Every balanced recipe in this book was formulated using software we built ourselves. Every value was checked and rechecked multiple times to ensure accuracy. Though we can't guarantee there are zero mistakes, we are certain that our nutrition calculator is better than anything available on the market to calculate nutrition facts for homemade dog food. Cedric and Edith are thriving on these recipes—as well as many that aren't fully balanced. Because they eat so many different things, we rarely give balance any consideration at all. Their diets give them beautiful soft coats, lean bodies, and boundless energy.

DOGGY DENTAL HYGIENE

Regular brushing helps keep your pup's teeth and gums healthier for longer. If you're not already brushing your dog's teeth, it's time to start!

What to use: Although there are now all sorts of options, from finger toothbrushes and specialized toothpaste to dental wipes and supplements, we opt to keep things simple and use coconut oil and a child's toothbrush.

When to do it: Find a schedule that works for you. If you can manage daily brushing, you're an A+ pup parent. If you can't and just manage to do it once or twice a week, your dog will still benefit.

Beyond brushing, chewing bones are great for cleaning teeth as well as jaw stimulation. We use 100 percent collagen chews made in the USA that are ethically sourced and traceable.

FAQs

When it comes to feeding, there are some questions we get asked a lot. Here are our answers.

How do you define real food, and why does my vet think it's dangerous?

Many people are confused about what is actually real food. Real, whole foods are unprocessed meats, veggies, fruits, grains, and fats. This is what we mean by feeding real food to dogs—we do not mean giving them part of your take-out pizza.

We don't consider many of the foods people eat, like fast food, junk food, and processed foods, to be an appropriate form of sustenance. These foods are not recommended for your dog. (We also don't think any person should be eating these regularly, either, but can't help an occasional indulgence ourselves.)

Although most veterinarians understand the distinction between "real food" and "food people eat," they don't have the time or the energy to explain things clearly. The protocols in the medical and veterinary fields are made to be as simple (and profitable) as possible. It's simpler for them to say that feeding real food is too complicated or dangerous. Recommending kibble (and telling you to pick some up on your way out) is just easier and better business than helping you come up with a meal plan. That's what this book is for.

How is real food better than kibble? Kibble is studied and approved by vets and regulatory bodies.

Most dog food is made by a process called extrusion. This process was developed in the 1950s to make foods cheaper and safer. High temperatures and high pressure kill bacteria and other pathogens, while the machine does all the work. In order for this process to happen, however, the dough that forms the kibble must have 40 percent or more of its calories from carbohydrate.

This means that refined carbohydrates are the single biggest ingredient in kibble.

In the veterinarian world you often hear about balance, but vets are usually referring only to micronutrients like vitamins and minerals. These things are easy to get with synthetic additives. Vets rarely talk about macronutrients—that is, carbs, fats, and proteins—because the balance of these in kibble is way off. In fact, studies on the glycemic response to commercial dog foods show that increasing the amount of refined carbohydrate is the primary factor contributing to elevated blood sugar, high insulin levels, and increasing obesity in dogs.[21]

Most dogs fed real food have a hard time going back to kibble; it's simply not made with what they need to thrive. This mismatch causes all sorts of issues like chronic inflammation, obesity, tooth decay, and skin and digestive irritation. Refer to the section on AAFCO balance, page 12, for more details.

Should dogs eat raw food?

Raw feeding is growing in popularity. Some of the comments on our videos are "Why not just feed the food to them raw?" or "Raw is best for dogs because that's how they ate in the wild."

Many pet parents find that their dogs thrive on raw diets, and for good reason. Real whole foods, even when raw, are still much better than highly processed kibble. Just like dogs, people can also eat raw food, but we usually don't eat exclusively raw for several reasons. It's for similar reasons that we give our dogs cooked food.

First, there are pathogens and parasites that live in all animals. Though dogs are more resilient to pathogens than people are, they can still get sick. Also, studies show that dogs who sometimes eat raw are about eight times more likely to shed pathogens in the home.[22] This is particularly risky in homes with small children and immunocompromised people. Most of the meat and poultry sold in stores is processed and handled for cooking. Different processes are applied for food meant to be eaten raw. For example, fish labeled "sashimi

grade" is typically frozen at temperatures low enough to kill parasites.

Second, cooking is an ancient technology that not only kills pathogens but also makes food more digestible. Cooked proteins are denatured in a way that makes them easier for the body to utilize. Also, cooking helps us extract nutrients from plants (neither dogs nor people can break down cellulose). Proponents of raw diets that include plants usually recommend blending or steaming them.

Furthermore, raw diets are more difficult to balance in terms of both macronutrients and vitamins and minerals. Raw feeders usually require supplements to meet dietary requirements.

Whether these nutrient deficiencies matter over time is still unclear. However, the idea that raw diets are *better* than lightly cooked diets is definitely not substantiated by any evidence, anecdotal or scientific. Conversely, many studies, as well as our own experience, suggest that raw is riskier. Also, archaeological records suggest that people have been cooking for over 100,000 years. So, it's likely that domesticated dogs have been eating cooked food for a very long time.

Doesn't real food cause diarrhea in dogs?

Real food does not cause diarrhea in healthy dogs. Rather, diarrhea occurs because the digestive systems of dogs that eat only kibble change to digest only kibble. The microbiome, enzymes, and acids in the digestive tract take on maladaptive traits. So, when a dog that's accustomed to dry kibble eats something new, the bacteria and digestive tract can overreact, causing an upset tummy. This is probably why so many people believe their dogs can't stomach anything other than dog food.

Some dogs, just like some people, may have naturally irritable digestive systems, but this is rare. Irritable bowel syndrome (IBS) occurs in 3–9 percent of the human population, with the figure depending on the study. The literature on dog IBS is sparse, but many of the studies on idiopathic diarrhea (those cases with no known cause) show that it can be resolved in most dogs with the addition of psyllium husk.[23] This suggests that most issues with dog digestion are related to the foods that they eat.

If your dog is sensitive to new foods, don't worry. This is very common. Start slowly and introduce new foods a little at a time. Eventually, you will find that most, if not all, of the issues your dog experiences will go away once they are eating an exclusively real-food diet.

Is saturated fat bad for dogs? What about cholesterol?

Saturated fats are fats that are solid at room temperature. They typically come from animals but are also found in some plants like coconuts and cacao. Because oil and water don't mix, our bodies create lipoproteins (also called cholesterols), which can bond to water and fat, in order to shuttle the fats around in the blood. Saturated fats in the human diet often increase low-density lipoproteins (LDLs), the type of cholesterol that is associated with cardiovascular disease (CVD). For dogs, cholesterol and saturated fats are less of an issue than they are for humans because dogs rarely die of CVD. Their ancestral diet likely had high amounts of animal fats. This is why fats and specifically animal fats are crucial components of a healthy diet for dogs. See "Dogs Need Fats," page 8, for more.

My vet says "human food" causes pancreatitis. Is this true?

"Human food" is *not* the cause of pancreatitis.

Pancreatitis is a common inflammatory disease in modern dogs. It affects the pancreas, the organ that regulates dogs' blood sugar and produces digestive enzymes. Researchers consider most cases of pancreatitis to be idiopathic, or without an identifiable cause.[24] Numerous factors are associated with pancreatitis, including diabetes mellitus, dietary habits, and genetics. However, because vets see an increase in illness over the holiday season (when dogs are more likely to get into the trash or eat table scraps), they use this as anecdotal evidence that dogs shouldn't have any real food. The reality is that cardiovascular incidents and deaths for people also spike during the holidays. By that logic, people probably shouldn't eat holiday food, either.

Though the term *pancreatitis* is thrown around a lot, the truth is that it is actually a very difficult condition to accurately diagnose. In a postmortem analysis of 200 dogs, researchers reported that chronic pancreatitis was observed in 34 percent of dogs that died of other causes.[25] In another case-controlled study on pancreatitis (case-controlled studies are weaker than randomized controlled studies), researchers calculated that the highest-risk activities are (1) having a major surgical procedure and (2) eating out of the trash. Furthermore, pancreatitis is quite difficult to diagnose in dogs because the symptoms of pancreatitis are similar to those of a number of other diseases. **And the most common test for pancreatitis has a false positive rate of up to 40 percent!**[26]

How can I tell if my dog is allergic to a certain food?

True food allergies in dogs are rarer than people believe. Food sensitivities can be caused by many factors, including allergies, poor digestion, microbiome reaction, and inflammation. One expert on allergies in dogs asserts that food *and* environmental allergies affect 10 percent of dogs.[27] For these reasons, most researchers assume that 5 percent or less of dogs have true food allergies.

If your pup has a bad reaction to a food, it's more likely to be an intolerance. For example, adult dogs do not produce enough enzymes to digest lactose, the sugar in milk. When a dog consumes too much milk, they often get bloated and have diarrhea. Another type of intolerance (such as fructose intolerance) occurs when the animal is unable to absorb the nutrient. Allergies, on the other hand, occur when an animal's immune system mistakes elements in the environment (usually proteins) for pathogens like bacteria, viruses, and fungi. Skin issues and dermatitis are often caused by environmental allergens.

How to Use This Book

The recipes in this book are organized into the following sections: "Adult Maintenance Recipes," "Special Diets," and "Meals for Foodie Pups." Our recipes range from simple and quick to gourmet dishes that give you a chance to practice your culinary skills.

Adult Maintenance Recipes

As the title of this section suggests, these are recipes intended to feed a healthy adult dog. We've divided this section into three categories: Basics, Balanced Meals, and Supermeals.

Basics: These recipes are made from six ingredients or fewer, all readily available from the supermarket. Although each recipe is not 100 percent balanced, they contain every essential nutrient required by dogs, but some in lower amounts than AAFCO recommends. Adult dogs can be fed these recipes for weeks at a time without any major issue (though it's not recommended). These recipes are a great way to get started, and after you've worked your way up to more complex fare, they can still be used as quick meals when you're in a pinch and need something to feed your dog. Eggs are a major component of these recipes because they are so rich in nutrients. If your dog has an egg sensitivity, try Hot Pawt, which uses oysters to replace some of the nutrients that eggs provide, or skip straight to the Balanced Meals.

Balanced Meals: These recipes are fully balanced to better than AAFCO standards. We incorporate fish for omega-3s and vitamin D, sea kelp for iodine, sunflower seeds for vitamin E, and oysters for zinc, copper, and selenium. Most of these recipes use eight ingredients or fewer and include grain-free and allergy-friendly options in the event that your dog has sensitivities or is one of the rare pups with allergies.

Supermeals: In this section we add more depth to your pup's palate by including a variety of fruits, grains, and veggies. We also explore more exotic proteins like duck and venison. You'll often see wheat germ listed as an ingredient; not only is it super nutritious, but it's a great alternative to sunflower seeds for vitamin E. Supermeals are high in essential nutrients and serve as a way to cultivate a more adventurous pup palate.

Special Diets

This section offers recipes for dogs at different points of their lives and with different nutritional needs.

Puppies and Mothers: Expectant mothers need slightly different nutrients based on the stage of gestation. The same is true for puppies. There are even differences between small- and large-breed puppies. We do our best to account for these differences and include different formulations for them. We add bonemeal and a little salt to account for the increased need for phosphorus and sodium. Every one of these formulations has added fish for growing brains and nervous systems.

Senior Dogs: Older dogs have slightly different dietary requirements than prime-age dogs. For these recipes we increase protein slightly while also reducing carbohydrates.

Athletes and Working Dogs: Depending on the type of activity that dogs are engaged

CHOOSE YOUR OWN CANINE CULINARY ADVENTURE

Whether you're just getting started or have been cooking for your pups for years, we think there's something for you in *The Dog's Table*. (After reading this book, you may not even need recipes at all and may feel comfortable formulating your own dog food. See "Dogs Need Micronutrients," page 11, to be sure they're getting what they need.) Here's how you can use this book.

Newbie: If you haven't made a meal for your dog before, we suggest starting with the Basic recipes. If you want to keep your dog on their current food, supplement with a Basic Meal once in a while until you and your dog are comfortable. You can also experiment with making your dog a treat, a dogtail (a dog cocktail), or a one-off special meal from the "Meals for Foodie Pups" section.

Intermediate: If you already feel comfortable making your dog's food but aren't exactly sure where to begin formulating, our Balanced Meals are a great place to start. If you're in a time crunch, just make a Basic Meal. But make sure to feed a Balanced Meal or Supermeal a few days per week.

Master Pup Chef: Once you're comfortable finding the ingredients for Balanced Meals and Supermeals, you can also experiment with formulating your own. Here is where you can start to use your intuition and learn more about what your dogs need to thrive. Look at the differences between the Basic Meals, Balanced Meals, and Supermeals, and understand how you might combine ingredients to make your own recipes. See "Dogs Need Micronutrients," page 11, to learn how we think about balance.

in, their diets will need drastically different formulations for optimal performance. Working dogs with constant low-to-mid-level output perform best on ultra-low-carbohydrate diets. Racing dogs, however, perform worse with similar diets and instead require more carbohydrates, with less protein and less fat.

Weight Loss: The literature suggests that low-carb, high-protein, high-fiber diets are best for weight loss. The recipes in this section also include psyllium husk to increase fiber content without adding any additional carbs from vegetables.

Meals for Foodie Pups

The last section of this book explores some of the fun dishes and treats you see on our channel. These dishes are created not with balance or everyday feeding in mind but rather as an experience for you to enjoy with your pups and family. These recipes are intended to be fun meals for special occasions, and treats for occasional feeding.

That's not to say that they have no health benefit: the recipes still call for wonderful whole-food ingredients. Plus, dogs love to smell and eat, so providing a sensory food experience for them enriches their lives.

Feeding Guide

How much should you feed your dog every day? There's no quick answer to this question; your dog's daily calorie needs depend on their size, breed, age, reproductive status, and activity level. (For instance, puppies need more than adult dogs of the same weight because their fast growth and development require more calories. Neutered and spayed dogs need about 20 percent fewer calories.) For healthy adult dogs, their weight is a good starting point. To give you a general idea of how much to feed, the feeding table on the next page provides *approximate* feeding guidelines for adult dogs (weight and calorie intake based on activity levels). Monitor your pup's weight and waistline to adjust up or down.

Weight	Daily Calorie Requirements		
	Low Activity	Medium Activity	High Activity
Up to 5 lb (2 kg)	140	175	225
10 lb (5 kg)	250	300	375
20 lb (9 kg)	500	575	650
30 lb (14 kg)	675	750	825
40 lb (18 kg)	875	950	1,050
50 lb (23 kg)	1,025	1,100	1,225
60 lb (27 kg)	1,200	1,300	1,410
75 lb (34 kg)	1,375	1,500	1,625
90 lb (41 kg)	1,600	1,750	1,900

Portioning our recipes for your dog

Once you know how many calories your dog should be getting each day, you can use that number to figure out how many meals each of our recipes will provide.

Each recipe lists an approximate calorie yield.

One way to calculate the number of portions a recipe makes is with math! Divide the recipe's calorie yield by your dog's daily calorie requirement to find out how many portions the recipe makes for your dog.

For instance, if your dog has a daily requirement of 300 calories and the recipe makes 3,000 calories, you divide 3,000 by 300 (3,000/300 = 10). This means the recipe will make 10 days' worth of food for your dog. Simply divide the dish into 10 portions (or 20 if you plan to split it into two meals a day) and store appropriately.

To skip the math, you can also estimate. In general, every cup of cooked food will have about 300 calories. Smaller dogs need about 1 cup of food per 10 pounds (5 kilograms) of body weight each day. Bigger dogs need about 1 cup of food for every 15 pounds (7 kilograms) of body weight.

These are just general guidelines. The most important factor is your dog's weight and body shape. Monitor their weight over time, and adjust their portion sizes up or down as necessary. Dogs will always act hungry, so don't base your feeding decisions on their devastatingly cute puppy eyes. Stay strong!

General good practices:

- Make sure your dog always has fresh, clean water to drink.
- Don't encourage your dog to engage in vigorous exercise right after meals. Instead, it's the perfect time for a nice nap!
- You know your dog best—if they are a speedy eater, forget to chew, or tend to choke, make sure you serve all food and treats in appropriate bite sizes for them or use a slow feeder.

Avoid overfeeding

Overfeeding in dogs (and humans for that matter) is the main driver of chronic disease. Cancer, heart disease, dementia, and diabetes are all related to metabolic health and body composition. If you want to keep your pup disease-free and spry for as long as possible, you'll want to keep them lean.

Feeding is rarely straightforward, so don't worry if it takes some time to get the hang of it. Some dogs are just more heavyset than others, even on limited diets. Most dogs will always look and act hungry. For healthier pups, limit their caloric consumption as best as you can. Of course, this doesn't mean that you should starve them. Feed on the lower side of their caloric guidelines and weigh them regularly. Even though it can be hard not to give in when it seems like more food makes your dog happy, they'll be happier in the long run when they are in good health as they get older. Here's how to check if your dog is a healthy weight:

- Stand above your dog for an aerial view of their body shape.
- You should be able to see a defined waistline and feel your dog's ribs slightly.
- Take pictures from above to document body shape change over time.

WHAT NOT TO FEED YOUR DOG

The list of foods that people *think* are toxic for dogs is really long. This (incorrect) list includes mushrooms, shrimp, avocados, bell peppers, tomatoes, peas, sweet potatoes, and more. Some of these are just mistaken beliefs, while others are actually a result of poor scientific research. For example, avocados have been reported to be toxic to dogs in many research papers—but when we did some digging to find out why, we found that most of that research cited one 2009 paper that had referenced a very low quality, anecdotal account of starving and neglected dogs from Kenya that lived near an avocado farm.[28] The fact that this paper became a primary source is a scientific travesty. Unfortunately, it is difficult to dispel myths that are already widely accepted as truth.

It's true that avocados contain persin, which can make dogs sick in large amounts, but it's concentrated in the skin and pit. The flesh doesn't have enough of it to be a concern. Toxic compounds naturally occur in small amounts in many foods, such as xylitol in berries, and solanine in tomatoes and potatoes. The good news is that the majority of foods we eat are also safe for dogs, and even the ones that are toxic require large amounts to make dogs really sick.

Here are some general rules about what to avoid:

1. Avoid feeding your dog parts of food you wouldn't eat, either: for example, cooked bones, shells, corncobs, peels, stems, seeds, and pits.

2. Avoid feeding your dog processed food, junk food, and fast food.

3. Very few ingredients that we know of are truly dangerous to dogs. These are outlined in the following chart.

Food	Toxic Substance Contained	Toxic Dose*	Lethal (Deadly) Dose*	Effects
Onions	Thiosulfate	Around 5 g/kg (onions)	Not well defined	Hemolytic anemia
Xylitol	Xylitol	As low as 0.1 g/kg	Approx. >1 g/kg	Hypoglycemia, liver failure
Macadamia nuts	Unknown	Approx. 2.4 g/kg	Not well defined	Hindlimb weakness, central nervous system depression
Grapes and raisins	Unknown	As few as one or two grapes/raisins	Not well defined	Acute renal failure
Chocolate	Theobromine	20–40 mg/kg theobromine	200 mg/kg theobromine	Central nervous system stimulation, cardiac issues
Ethanol	Ethanol	1–3 g/kg	5.5–7.9 g/kg	Central nervous system depression, hypothermia
Caffeine	Caffeine	140–200 mg/kg	190–240 mg/kg	Central nervous system stimulation, cardiac issues

*Doses are measured in milligrams or grams of toxin per kilograms of dog's body weight.

How to Prep Meals and Safely Store Food

As with any homemade food, it's important to follow food safety practices with your dog's meals. How you cool and store your dog's food is essential to preserving its freshness and quality.

As our recipes are all fresh, they are meant to be stored in the fridge and served ideally within four days.

For convenience, we love to make big batches and divide them into size-appropriate portions for Cedric and Edith. Portioning out the food before chilling or freezing makes it easy to grab and reheat a meal for your pup. As soon as the food is cooked, we place a few days' worth in the fridge for immediate consumption. We transfer the rest of the food to portion containers and place them in the freezer for easy feeding later. We suggest investing in portion containers that are freezer safe. Any airtight food containers, preferably glass, or silicone freezer trays with lids will work well for storing your pup's meals.

You can easily double or triple our daily recipes to make enough food for your dog to last a long time in the freezer. You can also halve or quarter them for small dogs, or if you just don't want to make as much.

To thaw a frozen meal before feeding, place it in the fridge until it softens. If we need a frozen block of food right away, microwaving, steaming, or gently heating on the stove works well.

What You Will Need

Cooking for your dog isn't revolutionary; it's basically the way that our companion animals have been eating since they started living with us. If you can cook a basic meal for yourself, you can do it for your dog. (And even if you think you *can't* cook a basic meal for yourself, cooking for your dog is easy—we promise!)

You don't need a lot of special items to make the most nutritious and healthy food for your pups. You probably already have most of the tools and ingredients, and you can get started with what's available right at the grocery store.

Most of our recipes can be made on the stove with basic tools—a cooking pot or pan, a spatula, and knives. Some of our recipes require a hand mixer, a food processor, or an oven. (A few of the recipes are easier to make with some specialty items: a sushi mat, a tamagoyaki pan, and a donut pan. These are completely optional, however.)

The ingredients we use will mostly be familiar to you, with just a few specialty items added for our Balanced and Supermeals recipes. Let's take a look.

Picking Good Produce

We generally go for local produce, grown by farmers in our area. We either shop at grocery stores that specialize in local produce or go to the farmer's market to get it directly from the people who grow it.

Our most commonly used vegetables are carrots, broccoli, beets, and sweet potatoes. Fruit isn't as much of a staple in our recipes, but we feed it daily as a snack on its own. **The dogs love bananas and**

blueberries. You'll also still see kiwi, apples, pineapple, and more in some of the recipes.

Our Favorite Grains and Seeds

Grains often get a lot of hate, but we find that our dogs do best when we include them in their diet (see "Do Dogs Need Carbohydrates?," page 10, for more). Grains give dogs energy, satiate their appetites, and help them form healthy poops and maintain their weight.

Rice, oats, and quinoa are common in many of our recipes. Although quinoa is not technically a grain (it's actually a seed), it can be used like one. Quinoa is highly nutritious and contains essential amino acids in addition to vitamins, minerals, and fiber. For rice we typically use the organic Haiga variety. This type of rice retains the germ, making it extra nutritious.

Sunflower seeds have one of the highest levels of vitamin E content. **Roasted, unsalted sunflower seeds** are best because roasting breaks down the cell walls to release the oil. Your dog may poop the seeds out whole, and while that is okay, you may prefer to crush them up before adding them to a recipe. The vitamin E oil mixes into the food when cooking.

Another great source of vitamin E, **wheat germ**, is used in many of the Supermeal recipes. It's the most nutritious part of the wheat plant and contains protein, fat, and essential micronutrients.

We Love Healthy Fats

Fats are an essential component of a nutritious doggy diet! See "Dogs Need Fats," page 8, for more. Most of the healthy whole-food proteins we use in these recipes (meats, poultry, seafood, dairy) naturally have some fat.

While you may be used to buying animal proteins for yourself (if you're not a vegetarian), one you may not be as familiar with yet is canned sardines. Small, oily fish like sardines are a great source of omega-3 fatty acids DHA and EPA, protein, vitamin D, and more. While DHA and EPA are not required by AAFCO, we believe they should be. **We use canned sardines in many of our recipes as they are highly nutritious, budget friendly, and easy to find.** While sardines are pretty bony, the canning process cooks the bones to a point where they are soft enough for your dog to eat. You can feed them the whole sardine, bones and all, directly from the can. We prefer using sardines canned in water with no added salt.

Our recipes also include healthy fats in the form of oils. Here are some of our favorite cooking fats:

- **Coconut oil:** High in saturated fats and medium-chain triglycerides (MCTs), coconut oil is both stable for cooking and a fast source of energy for dogs. We use it for frying, baking, brushing the dogs' teeth, and moisturizing their skin.
- **Olive oil:** High in monounsaturated fatty acids, olive oil appears in our everyday cooking, and we often drizzle extra-virgin olive oil on top of the dogs' food.
- **Beef tallow:** Tallow is high in saturated fats, so it's stable when cooking at high heat. We often use it for frying our own food.

❧ Clarified butter / grass-fed butter:
Butter is not your enemy and it's not your dog's enemy, either. Like tallow, clarified butter is more stable at high temperatures than vegetable oils. The dogs love a bite of cold butter as a snack, and we also use it to cook things like Pupcakes that just taste better cooked in butter.

Dog-Friendly Broth

Some of our recipes call for dog-friendly broth. Broth made for people often contains salt, onions, and spices. Although it is unlikely to harm your dog in limited quantities, making a batch especially for your pup is preferable. See "A Guide to Barking-Good Broth," page 60. For convenience, we like to keep bone broth powder or a few packs of store-bought broth in our pantry, too. Dog-friendly broths can be found at your local pet store or online.

Quality Proteins

Just as the food we eat affects our health, the food livestock eat affects their health as well. Several studies show differences in micronutrients in eggs from chickens raised with fortified feed.[29] Grain-fed beef and grass-fed beef also show differences in fatty acid profiles.[30] Similarly, there is a difference in nutrient profiles between wild-caught and farmed salmon.[31]

In general, we opt for wild-caught salmon and pasture-raised eggs. Grass-fed beef is great, but because much of the grass-fed beef in the United States is imported, we find it to be less ecologically friendly than locally grown, grain-finished beef. For both nutrition and ecological sustainability, the ideal beef for us is locally sourced grass-fed beef, but the supply is limited.

CANNED FOODS AND BPA

Bisphenol A (BPA) is a synthetic compound that helps make plastics more durable and heat resistant. It's often found in the lining of canned foods to protect the can from corrosion. In the late 1990s, researchers determined that BPA can mimic estrogen in the body. Later, low doses of BPA were linked to developmental, reproductive, and neurological effects in animals.[32] Despite health concerns, BPA is not regulated by the US government, but due to public pressure, many manufacturers are marketing products that are BPA-free or BPA-NI (BPA non-intent, meaning BPA is not intentionally added, but is not tested for). However, there is still concern that BPA alternatives, specifically BPS, BPF, and related compounds, may cause similar detrimental health effects.[33]

According to research conducted in Canada, BPA levels in canned seafood and canned soups have significantly decreased since 2014 and since 2017, respectively. However, similar trends were not observed for canned evaporated milk, luncheon meats, and vegetables, suggesting their continued use in industry.[34] When we use canned foods, we make sure to buy premium products labeled "BPA-free." Though we love canned sardines, we still limit them to only a few times per month. Fresh food is always best!

Farm-raised game meats like bison and venison are typically very lean and high in nutrients. They tend to be more expensive than more common proteins but are great for sensitive pups.

For fish, we prefer wild-caught ocean fish. Sardines, anchovies, small mackerel, and salmon all tend to be lower in environmental toxins. We avoid big-game fish, for example, swordfish and shark, while we sometimes feed fish like cod, snapper, and sablefish.

We avoid freshwater fish because the EPA reports that most of the freshwater fish tested in US waterways are above the threshold for mercury, which is 0.3 ppm (wild-caught salmon typically contain less than one-tenth of that level, 0.03 ppm or less). Also, all samples tested contained PFAS, the "forever" chemical found in Teflon.[35] Freshwater fish farmers use water from US waterways as their primary source. Though there are high-quality producers emerging, it's difficult for consumers to distinguish between them. We expect this to change in the future, but for now, we avoid freshwater fish.

Specialty Ingredients

These are the weirder ingredients you'll need to incorporate all the vitamins and minerals your dog needs. Now, if you don't have these on hand for a recipe, can you still make it?

Of course. However, if you're planning on cooking for your dog in the long term, then it would be wise to invest in these ingredients to make sure your dog is getting all the nutrients they need. You can easily find these items online.

- 🐾 **Sea kelp powder:** Sea kelp (*Ascophyllum nodosum*) powder is high in iodine, and we use it in our fully balanced recipes for this reason. Without it, it's hard to achieve the required iodine levels, unless you're using a synthetic source. (In the United States, table salt is iodized.) If you're going to be making all your dog's food, it's one of the few main things we recommend always keeping on hand. As a dried good, it will keep well for one to two years in an airtight container stored in a cool, dry pantry or even longer in the freezer. You only need to use a little bit at a time, so one pack will last you a long time.

- 🐾 **Oyster powder:** Another staple in our pantry, oyster powder is ground-up dried oysters. You will often see a ratio like 10:1 in the name. This just means that 10 ounces of fresh oyster is condensed down to 1 ounce of powder. Oysters are our source of zinc and selenium, as well as many other trace minerals. They are a nutrient powerhouse! Can you use

CONVERTING WET AND DRY INGREDIENTS

Most of our recipes call for one form of an ingredient like fresh veggies, dried grains, or freeze-dried beef liver. These recipe choices were made for simplicity. In the event you want to use a different form, let's say cooked rice instead of uncooked rice, here is a conversion chart. Amounts are approximate.

Grains 3:1	Cooked	Dry
Oats	3 cups / 270 g	1 cup / 90 g
Rice	1½ cups / 285 g	½ cup / 95 g
Quinoa	1 cup / 195 g	⅓ cup / 65 g

Freeze-Dried Meats 3.5:1	Fresh	Freeze-Dried
Beef liver	3½ oz / 100 g	1 oz / 30 g
Beef heart	1 lb / 454 g	5 oz / 150 g

Powders	Fresh	Powder
Oyster	2.8 oz / 80 g	1 tbsp (0.28 oz) / 8 g (10:1 extract)
Eggshell	1	5 g (¾ tsp)

Miscellaneous	1 Can	Fresh	Dry
Beans	15 oz / 425 g	1½ cups / 270 g (drained)	½ cup / 90 g (Never add dry beans directly to a recipe. They must be soaked overnight and cooked until tender first.)
Sardines	4¼ oz / 125 g	5 oz / 150 g	1.67 oz / 50 g

fresh oysters? Yes! But we find it more convenient to store and use powdered oysters. Freeze-dried or frozen oysters are good alternatives.

☙ **Eggshell:** Eggshell is also a staple ingredient in our recipes. It serves as a source of calcium. You can use fresh eggshells, as we do in many of our Basic recipes, but store-bought eggs are washed and sanitized before packing, meaning some chemical residue may remain. Wash fresh eggshells before using them. Generally, we prefer using ground eggshell as it's easy to store and the fine powder mixes into food seamlessly. You can also use a calcium supplement for all recipes

where eggshell is required. To figure out amounts, follow the directions on your supplement packaging rather than directly substituting 1:1 for ground eggshell.

☙ **Freeze-dried liver:** One of our hacks is stocking freeze-dried liver. It is much easier to find than fresh and keeps in a pantry for a long time. Liver is needed in many of our recipes to help fully balance them. Unfortunately, grocery stores don't always carry organ meat. The best solution is to hit your local pet store and buy a big pack of freeze-dried, human-grade liver. It is nearly as nutritious and you can cook it in most recipes the same way you would fresh liver.

Veggie-Free Beef Fricassee | 34

Adult Maintenance Meals

We created this first section of healthy real-food recipes with everyday feeding for adult dogs in mind. You'll find three categories here—Basics, Balanced Meals, and Supermeals—that you can choose based on your feeding goals and your comfort level in the kitchen. Each recipe lists the amount it yields in calories so you can portion up servings according to your dog's needs (for portioning guidance, see page 20).

Basics

So you want to make your dog's food, but maybe it's new to you, or you're short on time. This section contains our most basic recipes, which anyone can make. They are super quick to throw together and use fewer than six ingredients (not including water!) that can easily be purchased at any grocery store. But while the recipes may be basic, they're anything but boring. Whether your pup is a fan of Chinese takeout, American classics, or Middle Eastern fare, this section will have something they will love. With only five ingredients (and no chopping!), Veggie-Free Beef Fricassee is a great place to start.

These meals are more than enough to sustain your pup but may be short on some essential nutrients if fed for the long term. Though they are not 100 percent balanced, they are nutritious and fulfill many of AAFCO's nutrient requirements, so you can feel good about feeding them to your dog regularly. We believe that offering your dog *only* fully balanced recipes, where every single nutrient is accounted for in every meal, is unnecessary just like it is for people; see pages 12–14 for more. If you make these Basics the core of your dog's diet, simply offering one of our Balanced or Supermeals recipes a few times a week will cover the nutrients your dog needs in the long term.

But enough of that, let's get cooking!

Bison Barkshuka

MAKES 1,000 CALORIES

We love bison because it's extremely nutritious. Now it's also becoming easier to find, with many grocery stores stocking it right next to the beef. If you can't find it, simply substitute lean ground beef. This simple one-pot meal inspired by the North African egg dish shakshuka also features pumpkin, a source of soluble fiber that's great for your dog's microflora.

½ lb (227 g) ground bison

¼ cup (45 g) dry quinoa

1 cup (240 ml) water

½ can (7.5 oz / 212 g) plain pumpkin puree*

3 large eggs (retain 1 eggshell)

1 tbsp (15 g) olive oil

1. Combine the bison, quinoa, and water in a medium skillet with a lid.

2. Bring to a boil on medium-high heat, turn the heat down to low, close the lid, and simmer for 15 minutes, or until the quinoa is fully cooked. You can tell the quinoa is done when it has puffed up and turned translucent, save for the white "tail" around the edge.

3. Stir in the pumpkin puree.

4. Use your spatula to make three pockets in the sauce for the eggs to fit in. Crack the eggs into the pockets.

5. Wash and crush the eggshell using a blender, a mortar and pestle, or just your hands (the smaller the dog, the smaller the pieces), then sprinkle the crushed eggshell into the pot.

6. Cover the skillet and cook until the egg whites are set and the egg yolks are jammy, about 5 minutes. Turn off the heat and drizzle in the olive oil.

7. Let the Barkshuka cool slightly before portioning into servings for your dog. Store any leftover portions in airtight containers in the fridge for up to 4 days. Cool completely before serving.

*Double the recipe to use the entire can of pumpkin puree, or freeze the rest of it for next time.

Veggie-Free Beef Fricassee

MAKES 1,850 CALORIES

For the picky pups who spit out their vegetables, this veggie-free dish is mainly meat, eggs, and quinoa. With just four ingredients (not including water), it's a quick and easy way to feed a hungry pup.

1 lb (454 g) lean ground beef

½ cup (90 g) dry quinoa

3 cups (720 ml) water

5 large eggs (retain 1 eggshell)

2 tbsp (30 g) olive oil

1. Combine the beef, quinoa, and water in a 4-quart pot. Bring to a boil on medium-high heat, then turn down the heat to low, cover the pot, and simmer for 15 minutes.

2. Add the eggs to the pot and stir to combine.* Wash and crush the eggshell using a blender, a mortar and pestle, or just your hands (the smaller the dog, the smaller the pieces) and add them to the pot.

3. Close the lid and simmer for 4–5 minutes, or until the eggs are cooked and the quinoa is fully puffed up and has a white "tail" around the edge.

4. Let the fricassee cool slightly before drizzling in the olive oil and portioning into servings for your dog. Store any leftover portions in airtight containers in the fridge for up to 4 days. Cool completely before serving.

*Adding the eggs toward the end prevents overcooking them, making the final dish more nutritious.

Beef and Broccoli

MAKES 775 CALORIES WITHOUT RICE, 950 CALORIES WITH RICE

Does your pup give you the side-eye when you bring home takeout? This meat and veggie dish, inspired by the Chinese American stir-fry, will be your dog's new favorite weekday dinner. If you serve the beef and broccoli without rice, it will be grain-free, low-carb, and high-fiber, which can be ideal for dogs that need to lose a few pounds. Cedric and Edith prefer it served with rice for an extra satisfying meal.

¼ cup (50 g) uncooked rice, washed (optional)

½ lb (227 g) lean ground beef or thinly sliced steak

½ small head (4 oz / 120 g) broccoli, roughly chopped

1 tbsp (15 g) olive oil

3 large eggs (retain 1 eggshell)

1. If serving rice, cook the rice first according to the package directions.

2. While the rice is cooking, heat up a large pan on medium heat. Add the beef and cook for 1–2 minutes to let it release some fat; this will help everything cook without sticking.

3. Add the broccoli and toss to combine.

4. Add a generous splash of water to the pan and cover with a lid. Let the meat and broccoli steam together for 3–4 minutes, or until the meat has browned and the broccoli has softened.

5. Push the meat and broccoli to the side of the pan to open up some space for the eggs. Drizzle in the olive oil and then crack in the eggs. Wash and crush 1 eggshell using a blender, a mortar and pestle, or your hands (the smaller the dog, the smaller the pieces) and add the pieces to the pan. Scramble the eggs until they're just cooked, then toss to combine with the beef and broccoli.

6. Remove from the heat. Mix in the rice, or keep it separate to serve on the side.

7. Let everything cool slightly before portioning into servings for your dog. Store any leftover portions in an airtight container in the fridge for up to 4 days. Cool completely before serving.

Pork Pottage

MAKES 1,125 CALORIES

In America, pork has a bad reputation. Perhaps it's because some cuts are high in fat or because pork is often cured with questionable preservatives. Most pork chop cuts are actually quite lean, and in moderation, fresh pork can be a good way to mix it up for your pup. Not to mention that it's an easy-to-source protein for pups with chicken or beef allergies.

Pottage is a stew that originated in Europe during medieval times and combines meat, vegetables, and grains into a hearty and satisfying meal. Dogs have been our companions since long before medieval times, and—since pet food is a relatively recent invention—we're guessing medieval pups probably enjoyed their fair share of leftover pottage.

1 tbsp (15 g) olive oil, divided in half

½ lb (227 g) lean, boneless pork chop, chopped into bite-sized pieces

1 cup (150 g) frozen peas

½ cup (45 g) rolled oats

3 large eggs (retain 1 eggshell)

1½ cups (360 ml) water

1. Heat half of the olive oil in a pan over medium-low heat. Add the pork chop pieces and cook, turning occasionally, for 6–8 minutes, or until browned and cooked through. Remove from the pan and set aside.

2. Add the peas, oats, eggs, and water to the same pan. Wash and crush 1 of the eggshells using a blender, a mortar and pestle, or your hands (the smaller the dog, the smaller the pieces). Add it to the pan, reduce the heat to low, and bring to a simmer. Let the mixture bubble for 10 minutes, or until the oats are softened. You may need to add more water as the oats absorb it.

3. Remove from the heat and add in the rest of the olive oil. Stir in the cooked pork, or keep it separate to serve on top.

4. Let everything cool slightly before portioning into servings for your dog. Store any leftover portions in airtight containers in the fridge for up to 4 days. Cool completely before serving.

Quick version: Skip browning the pork and throw everything into a pot (remember to wash and crush your eggshell as directed) at once, bring to a boil, then cook on low for 12–15 minutes.

Surf and Turf Bowl

MAKES 1,500 CALORIES

This meal puts the bounty of both the land and sea in one bowl, to your dog's delight. We love wild-caught salmon because it's nutrient dense, low in mercury, and loaded with EPA and DHA, the essential omega-3s from the ocean. Feeding fish a few times per week ensures your pup has enough of these critical nutrients for brain and nerve health.

2 large eggs (retain 1 eggshell)

¼ cup (50 g) uncooked rice, washed

1 cup (120 g) green beans

½ cup (120 ml) water

2 tbsp (30 g) olive oil, divided

½ lb (227 g) lean steak, chopped into bite-sized pieces

½ lb (227 g) salmon fillet, chopped into bite-sized pieces

1. Crack the eggs into a bowl and set aside.

2. Wash and crush 1 eggshell using a blender, a mortar and pestle, or your hands (the smaller the dog, the smaller the pieces).

3. Add the eggshell, rice, green beans, and water to a small pot.

4. Bring to a boil on medium heat, turn the heat down to low, cover the pot, and simmer for 20 minutes. Turn the heat off and let the mixture continue to steam for 5–10 minutes.

5. Meanwhile, in a medium pan, heat a little bit of the olive oil. Lightly sear the beef cubes on low for 3 minutes. Transfer the beef to a large bowl and set aside.

6. In the same pan, add the salmon cubes and cook for 8–10 minutes, or until thoroughly cooked, opaque, and flaking apart. (Wild-caught salmon should not be fed to dogs raw or underdone.)

7. When the salmon is done, transfer it to the bowl with the beef. Pour the eggs into the same pan and cook until just set, about 3 minutes. Transfer the eggs to the bowl with the beef and salmon.

8. When the rice and green beans are done, fluff up the rice and transfer the mixture to the bowl with the beef, salmon, and eggs. Stir together with the rest of the olive oil.

9. Let everything cool slightly before portioning into servings for your dog. Cool completely before serving. Store any leftover portions in airtight containers in the fridge for up to 4 days.

White Bean Chicken Chili

GRAIN-FREE 🐾 MAKES 2,600 CALORIES

Lighter than traditional red chili, this white chili is a flavorful and hearty dish made with navy beans and poultry. This recipe is made to use up a whole can of beans, so it makes a big batch. Refrigerate 4 days' worth for your dog, then portion and pop the rest in the freezer. You may have heard that beans can cause disruption to doggy tummies, but the research suggests that this isn't true. Dogs fed diets of 25 percent cooked beans showed no disruption to their microbiome.[36]

2 lb (908 g) ground chicken or chopped chicken breast

1 (15 oz / 425 g) can no-salt-added navy beans, drained

3 cups (720 ml) water or unsalted chicken broth

8 large eggs (retain 2 eggshells)

2 tbsp (30 g) olive oil

Fresh basil or cilantro (optional)

1. Combine the chicken, beans, and water or broth in a large saucepan. Bring to a boil on medium-high heat, then reduce the heat to low and simmer for 8–10 minutes, or until the chicken is cooked.

2. Add the eggs and stir, combining them into the sauce. Wash and crush 2 eggshells using a blender, a mortar and pestle, or your hands (the smaller the dog, the smaller the pieces) and add them to the pan. When the eggs have just set, in about 1 minute if simmering, turn off the heat.

3. Stir in the olive oil.

4. Let the chili cool slightly before portioning into servings for your dog. If you like, top with fresh herbs before serving. Store any leftover portions in airtight containers in the fridge for up to 4 days. Cool completely before serving.

If you prefer to use dried beans (see conversion chart on page 27), follow the package instructions for soaking and thoroughly cooking them <u>before</u> you use them in a recipe. Never add dry beans directly to a recipe.

Turkey Patties

MAKES 10 SILVER-DOLLAR-SIZED PATTIES, 1,700 CALORIES

Meat patties are the ultimate format for your pup's meals if you appreciate convenience. They are grab-n-go and extra easy to store, freeze, thaw, and even transport for short trips or outdoor picnics.

1 lb (454 g) lean ground turkey

3 large eggs (retain 1 eggshell)

1 cup (120 g) finely chopped or grated carrots

1 cup (90 g) rolled oats

2 tbsp (30 g) olive oil

Chopped fresh mint, dill, or cilantro (optional)

1. In a bowl, combine the turkey, eggs, carrots, oats, and olive oil. Wash and crush 1 eggshell using a blender, a mortar and pestle, or your hands (the smaller the dog, the smaller the pieces) and add it to the bowl. Mix everything together until the ingredients are thoroughly combined.

2. Measure out ¼- or ½-cup (50 or 100 g) balls, depending on your preferred size, and flatten them into patties about ½ inch (1.5 cm) thick.

3. Heat up a skillet on medium-low heat. Cook the patties, pressing them down to ensure even cooking, for 3–5 minutes, or until browned on one side. Flip them over and cook on the other side for another 3–5 minutes, or until cooked through. (Tip: Splash a few tablespoons of water into the pan, and cover with a lid to steam them for even cooking.)

4. Let the patties cool slightly and sprinkle with herbs before portioning into servings for your dog. Break the patties into smaller pieces as needed before feeding. Cool completely before serving. As this is a drier meal, we recommend serving it with water (or a dogtail; see pages 284–285). Store any leftover portions in airtight containers in the fridge for up to 4 days.

Hot Pawt

GRAIN-FREE ❧ **MAKES 1,825 CALORIES**

When you have hot pot, you add a variety of fresh ingredients into a simmering broth to dip and cook as you eat. At the end of the meal, you'll have an extremely flavorful and nutritious soup from everything that went in it. Our doggy Hot Pawt takes inspiration from typical hot pot ingredients to create a version suitable for any lucky pup. If you plan on giving your pup the full Hot Pawt experience, please cool each item before serving.

2 cups (480 ml) water or dog-friendly broth

1 small (8.5 oz / 240 g) sweet potato, cubed

2 heads (7 oz / 200 g) baby bok choy

2 oz (60 g) fresh or frozen oysters

1 lb (454 g) lean lamb, thinly sliced

2 tbsp (30 g) olive oil

Optional Hot Pawt Ingredients for Your Inspiration
(choose a few)

Thinly sliced mushrooms such as enoki, shiitake, maitake, button, cremini, lion's mane (cooking time: 5–6 minutes)

Thinly sliced lotus root, carrots, bamboo shoots (cooking time: 5 minutes)

Beef slices, chicken liver chunks, chicken gizzards, beef heart, tripe, or your pup's favorites (cooking time: from 2 minutes for thin beef slices to 10 minutes for chicken liver chunks)

1. In a large pot over medium-high heat, bring the water or broth to a boil. Lower the heat to medium-low and bring to a simmer.

2. Add your ingredients in order of their cooking time, longest to shortest, and simmer until they're done. Sweet potato cubes will be fork-tender in about 10 minutes. Bok choy and oysters cook in 3–5 minutes, and thinly sliced lamb will be lightly cooked in 1–2 minutes.

3. Remove the Hot Pawt from the heat and drizzle the olive oil on top. Let everything cool slightly before portioning into servings for your dog. Serve with the broth, of course! Cool completely before serving. Store any leftover portions in airtight containers in the fridge for up to 4 days.

Chinese Braised Pork

GRAIN-FREE ✲ **MAKES 1,675 CALORIES WITHOUT RICE, 1,850 CALORIES WITH RICE**

This braised pork and egg dish is inspired by the Chinese dish hong shao rou, or soy sauce–braised pork. It's typically made with pork belly, but we use pork chops as they are much leaner. If you prefer, you can use beef or lamb stew chunks instead. Carob is optional but helps create that rich brown sauce that ties everything together. We use oyster powder here instead of organ meat to add critical nutrients. Serve on top of a small amount of freshly steamed rice, if you and your dog like.

¼ cup (50 g) uncooked rice, washed (optional)

1 lb (454 g) boneless lean pork chops, chopped into bite-sized pieces

1 small (8.5 oz / 240 g) sweet potato, chopped into bite-sized pieces

2 cups (480 ml) water or dog-friendly broth

1 tbsp (9 g) oyster powder (see chart on page 27 on how to sub fresh oysters)

½ tbsp carob powder (optional)

4 large eggs (retain 1 eggshell)

2 tbsp (30 g) olive oil

1. If serving rice, start cooking the rice according to the package directions.

2. Bring the pork, sweet potato, and water or broth to a simmer in a pot on medium-low heat. Stir in the oyster powder and carob powder (optional). Cover and cook for about 15 minutes, or until the sweet potato is soft.

3. While the pork and sweet potato cook, fill another pot with water and bring it to a boil on medium heat. Carefully add the whole eggs and boil for 5–7 minutes. Remove the eggs and immediately run them under cold water or transfer them to an ice bath. Peel the cooled eggs. Save and crush 1 of the eggshells.

4. Add the soft-boiled eggs and crushed eggshell to the pot with the pork and sweet potatoes.

5. Stir to coat everything in the sauce.

6. Remove the pot from the heat and stir in the olive oil. Let everything cool slightly before portioning into servings for your dog. Cool completely before serving. For smaller dogs, chop the boiled eggs into bite-sized pieces before serving. Store any leftover portions in airtight containers in the fridge for up to 4 days.

Quick version: Skip separately boiling the eggs, and crack them directly into the pot with the pork and sweet potatoes in step 2.

Egg Noodles

GRAIN-FREE 🐾 **MAKES 215 CALORIES**

These egg "noodles" are a low-carb replacement for regular noodles. We think your pup will love them even more, because of how nutrient dense eggs are compared to starchy noodles.

2 large eggs

½ tbsp (7 g) coconut oil

Method 1

1. Whisk the eggs in a small bowl.

2. Heat a large pan over medium heat, add the coconut oil, and gently heat it up.

3. Pour in the eggs and tilt the pan to coat it completely.

4. Let the eggs cook like one big pancake. When the eggs have mostly firmed up, flip the egg over and cook for a few more seconds until the other side is cooked. (Tip: If you're not confident with flipping, simply cover the pan and cook for 1–2 minutes to steam the top instead.)

5. Transfer the egg to a cutting board. Roll it up and slice crosswise into noodle strands.

6. Let the egg noodles cool completely before serving to your dog or using in another recipe.

Method 2

1. Whisk the eggs in a small bowl.

2. Preheat a griddle to low. Grease lightly with the coconut oil.

3. Transfer the whisked eggs to a squeeze bottle with a small nozzle.

4. Draw long strands onto the griddle horizontally to form "noodles."

5. Draw as many as you can and work quickly.

6. Let the strands cook for 30 seconds, or until just set, and then use a silicone spatula to slide them off the griddle. Transfer to a plate.

7. Let the egg noodles cool completely before serving to your dog or using in another recipe.

Method 1

Method 2

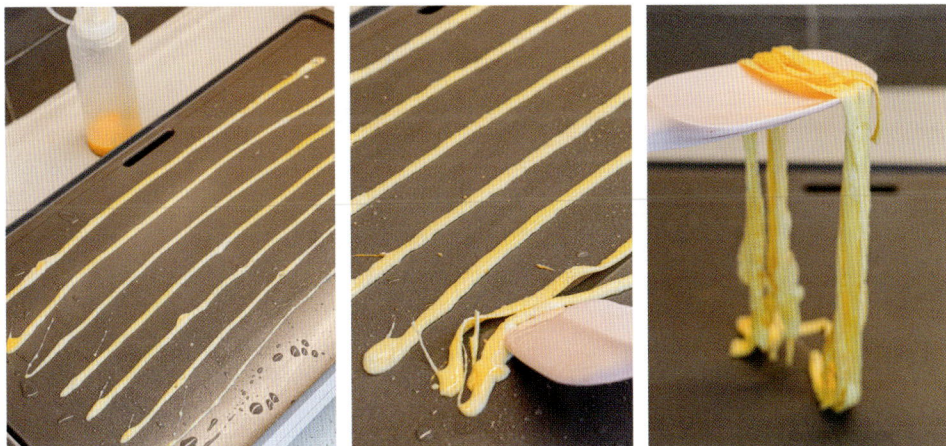

Chicken Pup Thai

MAKES 800 CALORIES WITHOUT OPTIONAL TOPPINGS

This dish is a fun take on pad thai, using egg strips as noodles. If you don't want to make the egg "noodles," simply scramble the eggs directly into the dish instead.

¼ cup (45 g) dry quinoa

½ lb (227 g) chicken, ground or finely chopped

½ cup (60 g) thinly sliced carrots

½ cup (120 ml) water

1 batch Egg Noodles (page 50) and 1 eggshell, or 2 large eggs (retain 1 eggshell)

1 tbsp (15 g) olive oil

Optional Toppings

2–3 pieces cooked shrimp

Thai basil

Cucumber

Hemp seeds

1. In a large pot over medium heat, combine the quinoa, chicken, carrots, and water.

2. Wash 1 eggshell and crush it using a blender, a mortar and pestle, or your hands (the smaller the dog, the smaller the pieces) and add them to the pot.

3. Bring to a simmer, reduce the heat to low, and cook for 12 minutes, or until the quinoa is puffed up.

4. Toss the egg "noodles" in with the mixture. If you didn't make the noodles, simply add the raw eggs now and scramble them into the mix. Remove from the heat and drizzle olive oil.

5. Let the Pup Thai cool slightly before portioning into servings for your dog. Cool completely before serving. Top with the optional cooked shrimp, basil, cucumber or hemp seeds. Store any leftover portions in airtight containers in the fridge for up to 4 days.

SPUP

MAKES 1,800 CALORIES

SPAM is widely loved and widely hated. If you grew up eating it, you probably love it like we do—but as it's highly processed, it's only an occasional treat for us now, and not something we'd share with the dogs. This dog-friendly SPUP can be steamed or baked and is great for dogs that don't chew so well. It's also simple to slice and store.

1 lb (454 g) ground turkey

3½ oz (100 g) fresh chicken liver

1 cup (120 g) chopped carrots (about 2 medium carrots)

4 large eggs (retain 1½ eggshells)

1 cup (90 g) oats

½ cup (120 ml) water

1 tbsp (15 g) olive oil

1. In a blender or food processor, combine the turkey, liver, carrots, eggs, washed eggshells, oats, water, and olive oil. Pulse until you have a paste.

2. Transfer the mixture to a loaf pan or baking dish. The SPUP will cook faster in a shallower dish and will take slightly longer in a deeper dish.

- To bake: Bake in a 350°F (175°C) oven for 50 minutes to 1 hour, or until the internal temperature reaches 165°F (75°C).

- To steam: Fill a steamer pot with water and bring to a rolling boil over medium-high heat. Place a heat-safe dish with your SPUP in the steamer and steam for 30–40 minutes, or until the internal temperature reaches 165°F (75°C).

3. Let the SPUP rest for 10 minutes before slicing, then let it cool slightly before portioning into servings for your dog. Cool completely before serving. Store any leftover portions in airtight containers in the fridge for up to 4 days.

Puptato Gratin Pie

GRAIN-FREE 🐾 **MAKES 1,850 CALORIES**

This dish fuses the famous potatoes au gratin, a dish of layered potatoes, with a shepherd's pie. The result is kind of like a potato lasagna, with layers of saucy meat and sweet potatoes.

1 lb (454 g) 90% lean ground beef or bison

1 (14 oz / 425 g) can plain pumpkin puree

4 large eggs (retain 1 eggshell)

2 tbsp (30 g) olive oil

1 small (8.5 oz / 240 g) sweet potato, thinly sliced into rounds

1 sprig rosemary (optional)

1. Preheat the oven to 350°F (175°C).

2. Combine the beef, pumpkin puree, eggs, and olive oil in a bowl. Wash and crush the eggshell using a blender, a mortar and pestle, or your hands (the smaller the dog, the smaller the pieces) and add it to the bowl. Mix everything together until thoroughly combined.

3. Layer the pie: Spread half the beef mixture into an 8-inch (20-cm) square baking pan, then layer half the sweet potato slices on top. Add the rest of the beef mixture, then top with the remaining sweet potato slices and a sprig of rosemary if you like.

4. Bake for 45–55 minutes, or until bubbling and golden.

5. Let the pie cool slightly and remove the rosemary before portioning into servings for your dog. Cool completely before serving. Store any leftover portions in airtight containers in the fridge for up to 4 days.

Bad Belly Soup

GRAIN-FREE ☙ MAKES 120 CALORIES

All pup parents have probably experienced their dog getting an upset stomach. Tummy issues happen for both people and dogs, and we can all agree that they're no fun. Whether your pup caught a bug at the dog park or ate something out of the trash, always check in with your vet to see if medical intervention is needed. If your pup is prescribed a few days of rest and bland food to recover, make them this gentle soup to help keep them hydrated and nourished.

In studies of idiopathic (no identifiable cause) diarrhea, 90 percent of dogs responded positively to psyllium husk, an important ingredient in this recipe.

2 cups (480 ml) dog-friendly broth

½ cup (60 g) chopped butternut squash or pumpkin

1 egg

½ tsp (1 g) psyllium husk

1. In a small pot over medium heat, bring the broth to a boil.

2. Add the squash or pumpkin, reduce the heat to low, and simmer for 15–20 minutes, or until past fork-tender.

3. Crack in the egg and whisk to combine.

4. Cook for 2 minutes, then turn off the heat. Stir in the psyllium husk.

5. Cool completely before serving. Serve one-quarter of your dog's normal portion size; wait 1 hour before feeding a little more if they seem well. Store any leftover soup in the fridge for up to 3 days.

This recipe is not nutrient dense enough to serve for more than a few days. Go back to regular food as soon as your pup can tolerate it. Seek proper medical attention as needed.

A GUIDE TO BARKING-GOOD BROTH

Quick meat broths and long-simmered bone broths are great additions to your dog's diet (and yours, too)! The long simmering time of bone broth allows nutrients more time to dissolve into the water. Protein, fats, and vitamins are all more concentrated in long-simmered broth. That said, even quick broths are a good source of hydration, plus your dog will love the added flavors and aromas.

There's no specific recipe for making a barking-good broth, but we offer some basic guidelines that can be customized depending on what foods you want to use. You'll need meat bones and (optionally) some veggies and herbs. Here are our suggestions:

- 🐾 Grass-fed beef is great. There is some research showing that micronutrient profiles in grass-fed meat can be more favorable, with more omega-3s (see "Dogs Need Fats," page 8).
- 🐾 Chicken feet are a worthy addition—they're high in collagen.
- 🐾 You don't need to stick with meat and bones from just one animal; using a combination can bring depth of flavor.

A good starting ratio is 10 parts water to 5 parts meaty bones to 2½ parts veggies. For example, this would be 2 quarts of water to 2 pounds of meaty bones to 1 pound of veggies, or (this is where the metric system is more helpful) 2 liters of water to 1 kilogram of bones to 400 grams of veggies.

Meat Bones

For chicken broth: chicken feet, drumsticks, a stewing hen, chicken bones

For turkey broth: turkey bones, turkey legs, turkey feet

For beef broth: beef bones, beef marrow bones, beef ribs

For pork broth: pork bones, pork knuckle, ribs

Optional Vegetables

Carrots, celery stalks, shiitake mushrooms, goji berries, dried dates, sliced fresh ginger, or herbs like rosemary or thyme

Quick Meat Broth

1. Use any meat and vegetables.

2. Put the ingredients in a big pot and cover with water. Simmer on medium-low for at least 20 minutes.

3. Strain out the meat and veggies and let the broth cool before serving it to your dog. Store any leftover broth in airtight containers in the fridge for up to 4 days. Meat and veggies can be fed with or separately from the broth.

Bone Broth

1. Use mostly bones, meaty bones and vegetables.

2. Place the meat and bones in a large pot of cool water and bring to a boil over medium-high heat.

3. Once the pot has boiled, drain and rinse the meat and bones with cool water, removing any of the proteins and grime.

4. Return the bones to the pot, cover with clean water, and bring to a boil over medium-high heat.

5. Cover, lower the heat, and simmer for 8–12 hours, replenishing the water if the level of liquid gets too low.

6. In the last 1–3 hours, add veggies of choice and continue to simmer.

7. Strain out the meat and veggies and let the broth cool before serving it to your dog. Store any leftover broth in airtight containers in the fridge for up to 4 days.

Balanced Meals

If you are looking for fully balanced dog meals, these are the recipes for you. These meals meet or exceed all of AAFCO's nutrient requirements for dog food manufacturers. Each recipe also passed the Cedric and Edith review board, though that board may be biased as they approve everything we make. These dishes can be fed daily or used to supplement a diet made up of the Basic recipes.

Recipes in this section call for a few more ingredients than our Basic Meals do, but the number of items needed is generally limited to 10. Here we add ingredients like beef liver, sunflower seeds, and fish, and nearly every recipe calls for sea kelp and oyster powder. You can substitute 2.8 oz / 80 g of fresh oysters for every 1 tbsp oyster powder. We use ground eggshell powder instead of fresh eggshells, simply because it's neater. If you choose to continue to use crushed whole eggshells rather than ground, substitute 1 fresh eggshell for every ¾ tsp (5 g) ground eggshell.

You might wonder, *Can I still make the recipe if I don't have all the ingredients?* Yes! While substituting or omitting ingredients changes the balance, that's okay as a one-off or even a short-term solution. For example, most Balanced Meals call for liver because it's needed in many recipes to meet AAFCO guidelines. Do dogs *need* liver every day? No, they don't. Just make sure to include the missing ingredients a few times a week for the long-term health of your dog.

Hungry Edith's Meatloaf

MAKES 1,810 CALORIES

This quinoa-and-beef-based meatloaf was Edith's first meal after coming home from the shelter. She promptly devoured it! It soothed her anxious tummy and helped improve her digestion. Since then, it has remained a favorite because it is so easy to prepare—just mix all the ingredients in a big bowl, pop it in your baking dish, and bake. (If you have a food processor, you can just toss in the veggies whole and you won't even have to chop.)

This dish is fully balanced per AAFCO standards but is a bit short on omega-3s DHA and EPA (AAFCO doesn't require DHA and EPA). We recommend feeding fish oil, krill oil, or adding a meal with fish a few times per week.

1 lb (454 g) lean ground beef

1½ cups (6 oz / 180 g) finely chopped carrots (about 3 medium carrots)

1 cup (125 g) green beans, diced for smaller dogs

½ cup (90 g) dry quinoa

1 cup (240 ml) water

4 large eggs

⅓ oz (9 g) freeze-dried beef liver

3 tbsp (26 g) roasted, unsalted sunflower seeds

1 tbsp (9 g) oyster powder

¾ tsp (5 g) ground eggshell

½ tsp (1 g) sea kelp powder

1. Preheat the oven to 350°F (175°C).

2. Combine all the ingredients in a large bowl or food processor and mix thoroughly.

3. Transfer the mixture to a casserole dish, dutch oven, or any oven-safe pot with a lid. Smooth the mixture out into one even layer.

4. Cover and bake for 1 hour to 1 hour and 15 minutes, or until the internal temperature reaches 165°F (75°C) and the quinoa has cooked all the way through.

5. Let the meatloaf cool slightly before portioning into servings for your dog. Cool completely before serving. Store any leftover portions in airtight containers in the fridge for up to 4 days.

Steak Bowl

MAKES 1,000 CALORIES

We have Chipuptle at home, ladies and gentledogs! Your pup will go wild for this grilled steak bowl, especially if you get the perfect rare cook on that steak. This meal, lower in carbs and higher in protein than other Balanced Meals, makes about 1,100 calories with bison. If you're using beef, this recipe will be a little higher in fat and higher in calories, while slightly lower in protein.

¼ cup (45 g) dry quinoa

¼ oz (7.5 g) freeze-dried beef liver chunks

1 tbsp (9 g) roasted, unsalted sunflower seeds

¼ cup (25 g) chopped spinach

½ cup (120 ml) water

½ lb (227 g) bison steak or beef steak

1 tbsp (15 g) olive oil

½ tsp (3 g) ground eggshell

½ tsp (1 g) sea kelp powder

1 (4¼ oz / 125 g) tin unsalted sardines in water, drained

½ cup (75 g) chopped cucumber

Fresh herbs, microgreens, or avocado (optional)

1. In a small pot over medium heat, combine the quinoa, beef liver, sunflower seeds, spinach, and water. Bring to a boil, turn down the heat to low, cover, and simmer for 12–15 minutes, or until the quinoa has fully expanded.

2. While the quinoa cooks, in a separate pan or on a grill, sear each side of the steak for 2–4 minutes, remove from the pan, and let it rest. It should be on the rare side.

3. Remove the quinoa from the heat and stir in the olive oil, ground eggshell, and kelp powder.

4. Slice the steak into pieces that your dog can easily eat. Let everything cool before portioning servings for your dog. Plate everything together—including the sardines, cucumbers, and optional ingredients—and serve. Store any leftover portions in airtight containers in the fridge for up to 4 days.

Turkey Chili

GRAIN-FREE, HYPOALLERGENIC 🐾 **MAKES 1,800 CALORIES**

This Turkey Chili is a twist on the classic, and extremely quick to make. You can feed your poor, starving dog (they are so good at that act, aren't they?) in just 20 minutes with this recipe. The black beans make it a satisfying meal without the grains. Don't want to use beans? Swap them out for ½ cup (90 g) dry quinoa.

1 lb (454 g) ground turkey

1 (15 oz / 400 g) can unsalted black beans, drained

1 oz (30 g) salmon

1 (15 oz / 425 g) can plain pumpkin puree

½ oz (15 g) freeze-dried bison or pork liver, crushed or in small chunks

3 tbsp (45 g) olive oil

2 tbsp (17 g) roasted, unsalted sunflower seeds

1 tbsp (9 g) oyster powder

¾ tsp (5 g) ground eggshell

½ tsp (1 g) sea kelp powder

1. Combine all the ingredients in a large pot and add just enough water to cover.

2. Bring to a boil on medium heat, turn the heat to low, and simmer for about 15 minutes, or until the meat is cooked through.

3. Let the chili cool slightly before portioning into servings for your dog. Cool completely before serving. Store any leftover portions in airtight containers in the fridge for up to 4 days.

If you prefer to use dried beans, follow the package instructions for soaking and thoroughly cooking them <u>before</u> you use them in a recipe. Never add dry beans directly to a recipe.

Loaded Pawchos

GRAIN-FREE 🐾 **MAKES 1,800 CALORIES**

Have you ever ordered nachos only to be served a plate of mostly chips and beans? Well, this recipe *doesn't* skimp on the meat! Our Pawchos are made from sweet potatoes instead of tortilla chips and are loaded with turkey and other toppings that make it a complete meal for your pup. Use any type of sweet potato, or even a combination, for colorful, nutrient-rich "chips."

1 small (8.5 oz / 240 g) sweet potato, sliced into thin circles

2 tbsp (30 g) olive oil

1 lb (454 g) lean ground turkey

1 cup (150 g) frozen peas

1 oz (30 g) salmon, chopped into bite-sized pieces

3 oz (90 g) fresh chicken liver

3 tbsp (26 g) roasted, unsalted sunflower seeds

1 tbsp (9 g) oyster powder

¾ tsp (5 g) ground eggshell

½ tsp (1 g) sea kelp powder

3 tbsp (45 g) plain yogurt or kefir, for drizzling on top (optional)

1. Preheat the oven to 350°F (175°C).

2. Layer the sweet potato circles on a coconut oil–greased or parchment-lined baking sheet.

3. Bake for about 20 minutes, or until fork-tender.

4. While the potatoes bake, heat a pan on medium-low and drizzle in the olive oil. Add the turkey, peas, salmon, liver, and sunflower seeds, and cook, stirring and breaking up the meat with a spoon, for 5 minutes, until the turkey is cooked through and the veggies have softened.

5. Remove from the heat and stir in the oyster powder, ground eggshell, and sea kelp powder.

6. When the sweet potato slices are done, layer the topping over them. Cool completely before portioning and serving. Optionally, drizzle yogurt or kefir on top. Store any leftover portions in airtight containers in the fridge for up to 4 days.

Chicken Adogbo

MAKES 1,800 CALORIES

Chicken adobo is the unofficial national dish of the Philippines and inspired our Adogbo, one of Cedric's all-time favorite meals. This recipe braises chicken and liver in a rich carob sauce to make a meal that even the pickiest pups won't be able to resist. If you can find quail eggs, they are the perfect size for smaller pups to enjoy.

½ cup (95 g) uncooked rice, washed

3 large eggs or 12 quail eggs

1 lb (454 g) chicken thighs, chopped into bite-sized pieces

1 oz (30 g) salmon, chopped into bite-sized pieces

3½ ounces (100 g) fresh chicken liver, chopped into bite-sized pieces

2 tbsp (17 g) roasted, unsalted sunflower seeds, crushed

1 tbsp (9 g) oyster powder or 3 oz (90 g) fresh or frozen oysters

2 tsp (6 g) carob powder (optional; see tip)

1 tsp (6 g) ground eggshell

1 cup (240 ml) water

1 tsp (2 g) psyllium husk (optional)

½ tsp (1 g) sea kelp powder

2 tbsp (30 g) olive oil

¼ cup (35 g) steamed peas and carrots (optional)

1. Prepare the rice in a rice cooker or on the stove according to the package directions.

2. Fill a pot with water and bring it to a boil on medium heat. Carefully add the whole eggs and boil (4–7 minutes for chicken eggs or 2–4 minutes for quail eggs). Remove the eggs and immediately run them under cold water or transfer them to an ice bath. Peel the cooled eggs.

3. In a deep pan or pot, combine the chicken, salmon, chicken liver, crushed sunflower seeds, oyster powder or oysters, carob powder (if using), ground eggshell, and water.

4. Bring to a boil on medium-high heat, turn the heat to low, and simmer for 10–15 minutes, or until the chicken is cooked through. If the pan is dry, add another 1 cup (240 ml) water. You want a saucy consistency.

5. Add the psyllium husk (if using). This helps to thicken the sauce.

6. Remove the pan from the heat and stir in the boiled eggs, sea kelp powder, and olive oil.

7. Let the Adogbo cool slightly before portioning into servings for your dog. Cool completely before serving. Serve with rice mixed in or on the side and an optional side of your dog's favorite steamed veggies. Store any leftover portions in airtight containers in the fridge for up to 4 days.

Tip: Add more carob powder to achieve that beautiful rich brown sauce!

Chicken Barkyani

MAKES 1,325 CALORIES WITHOUT RICE, 1,510 CALORIES WITH RICE

This highly aromatic Indian-inspired rice dish will leave your dog's nose buzzing. Some of the spices in the original dish, like turmeric and cinnamon, are also beneficial for pups. We've used a combination of cauliflower rice and basmati rice in this recipe. If you prefer to keep it grain-free, simply omit the rice.

2 tbsp (30 g) olive oil

1 lb (454 g) ground chicken or thigh pieces, chopped into bite-sized pieces

1¾ ounces (50 g) fresh chicken liver, chopped into bite-sized pieces

1 (4¼ oz / 125 g) tin unsalted sardines in water, drained

1 tbsp (9 g) roasted, unsalted sunflower seeds

⅛ tsp (0.5 g) ground turmeric

⅛ tsp (0.5 g) Ceylon cinnamon

1 tbsp (9 g) oyster powder

¾ tsp (5 g) ground eggshell

½ tsp (1 g) sea kelp powder

2 cups (200 g) riced cauliflower

1 cup (100 g) chopped spinach

¼ cup (50 g) uncooked basmati or other rice, washed (optional)

1 cup (240 ml) water

1 sprig cilantro (optional)

1. In a large saucepan or pot, drizzle the olive oil and heat on medium. Add the chicken and chicken liver and cook for 5–6 minutes, until nearly cooked through.

2. Add the sardines, sunflower seeds, turmeric, cinnamon, oyster powder, ground eggshell, and sea kelp powder. Toss to combine everything evenly.

3. Add the riced cauliflower, spinach, rice (if using), and water. Bring to a simmer, then cover with a lid. Cook for 15–18 minutes to let the rice expand. Check on the rice toward the end of the cooking time and add more water if needed.

4. Let the Barkyani cool slightly before portioning into servings for your dog. Optionally, top with a sprig of cilantro. Cool completely before serving. Store any leftover portions in airtight containers in the fridge for up to 4 days.

Chicken Pup Pie

MAKES 1,750 CALORIES

This delicious pup potpie will have your mouth watering, too, because it's just that good. We fully support your taking a bite.

Filling

1 lb (454 g) chicken thighs, chopped into bite-sized pieces, or ground chicken

2 cups (270 g) frozen peas and carrots

3½ oz (100 g) fresh chicken liver, chopped into bite-sized pieces

1 tbsp (9 g) oyster powder

1 oz (30 g) salmon

¾ tsp (1 g) ground eggshell

½ tsp (1 g) sea kelp powder

2 tbsp (17 g) roasted, unsalted sunflower seeds

½ cup (120 ml) water

Crust

1 cup (100 g) oat flour

1 tbsp (15 g) melted beef tallow or olive oil

2 large eggs

1. Preheat the oven to 350°F (175°C).

2. Combine all the filling ingredients in a large pot. Cook on medium heat, stirring to ensure the filling doesn't stick to the pot, for about 10 minutes, or until the chicken is just done. If the pan is dry, add another ½ cup (120 ml) water. If the filling is on the soupy side, add 1 tbsp (7 g) of the oat flour to it and cook for 2–3 minutes to thicken the mixture.

3. Make the crust: In a separate bowl, whisk up the remaining oat flour with the tallow or olive oil and eggs. The mixture should have the texture of a very thick cake batter, bordering on a paste. Add splashes of water if needed to bring it to the right consistency.

4. Transfer the pie filling to a 9-inch (24-cm) pie pan.

5. Pour or spread the batter on top in one even layer. It's okay if some of the filling peeks through.

6. Bake for 25 minutes, or until bubbly and golden brown.

7. Let the pie cool slightly before portioning into servings for your dog. Cool completely before serving. Store any leftover portions in airtight containers in the fridge for up to 4 days.

Quick, no-crust version: Combine all the filling ingredients in a pot, along with 1 cup (90 g) rolled oats (instead of oat flour) and eggs. Simmer on low heat for 15 minutes, or until the chicken is cooked through and the oats are softened.

Clay Pawt Rice

MAKES 1,300 CALORIES

Mushrooms are often said to be toxic for dogs. Not only are they not toxic, but they're extremely beneficial. Even so, you should only feed your dog store-bought mushrooms. Wild or foraged mushrooms can be dangerous for both you and your pup. As for preparation, cooking mushrooms thoroughly is always best.

1 tbsp (15 g) olive oil

1 lb (454 g) boneless, skinless chicken thighs, chopped into bite-sized pieces

3½ oz (100 g) fresh chicken liver

1 cup (80 g) cremini or shiitake mushrooms, thinly sliced

1½ oz (45 g) salmon, chopped into bite-sized pieces

¼ cup (50 g) uncooked rice, washed

½ cup (120 ml) water

1 tbsp (9 g) oyster powder

¾ tsp (5 g) ground eggshell

½ tsp (1 g) sea kelp powder

2 heads (7 oz / 200 g) baby bok choy, chopped

1. Heat the olive oil in a pot with a lid on medium-low heat. Add the chicken, chicken liver, mushrooms, and salmon and cook for 5 minutes, or until the chicken begins to brown (it doesn't need to be fully cooked yet).

2. Stir in the rice, water, oyster powder, ground eggshell, and sea kelp powder and bring to a boil. Cover with the lid, reduce the heat to low, and simmer for 15 minutes.

3. Add the bok choy on top, cover the pot, and continue cooking for another 5–6 minutes, or until the water has fully absorbed, the rice is fluffy, and the bok choy has softened.

4. Let everything cool slightly before portioning into servings for your dog. Cool completely before serving. Store any leftover portions in airtight containers in the fridge for up to 4 days.

Chicken Doodle Soup

MAKES 1,500 CALORIES

This soup is a feel-good meal that will be sure to uplift your dog's spirit on a cold and rainy day. Smelling it cooking in the house will warm up your soul, too!

We call for pasta in this recipe, but you can substitute quinoa if you prefer. These days, you can also find pasta made from rice, quinoa, lentils, chickpeas, and other wheat-free alternatives in most grocery stores. These options are great if your dog is sensitive to wheat. If you're feeling up to it, you can even make a batch of homemade Pawsta (page 197) or, for a grain-free option, Egg Noodles (page 50).

1 lb (454 g) chicken breasts or thighs, left whole

2 oz (60 g) chicken liver

1 cup (120 g) cubed carrots

2 cups (480 ml) water

1 oz (30 g) salmon

½ cup (50 g) chopped spinach

⅓ cup (65 g) dry pasta or quinoa

2 tbsp (17 g) roasted, unsalted sunflower seeds

½ tsp (1 g) sea kelp powder

1 tbsp (9 g) oyster powder

¾ tsp (5 g) ground eggshell

2 tbsp (30 g) olive oil

1. Add the chicken, chicken liver, carrots, and water to a pot and bring to a boil on medium heat. Cook for 10 minutes, or until the chicken is cooked through, then transfer the chicken to a plate using a slotted spoon.

2. Add the salmon, spinach, pasta or quinoa, sunflower seeds, sea kelp powder, oyster powder, and ground eggshell to the pot. Cover and cook on low for 10–15 minutes, or until the pasta or quinoa is done. Add more water if needed to cover everything.

3. Shred the chicken and return it to the pot. Stir to combine all the ingredients and give them one last minute to cook together. Remove from the heat and drizzle on the olive oil.

4. Let the soup cool slightly before portioning into servings for your dog. Cool completely before serving. Store any leftover portions in airtight containers in the fridge for up to 4 days.

Lion's Head Soup

MAKES 1,950 CALORIES

This famous Chinese dish, often served during holidays and family gatherings, is one of the favorite childhood dishes of Cedric and Edith's mom, Joelle. Giant, tender pork meatballs are cooked in a thick broth. The meatballs are said to look like lions' heads, which is the inspiration for the dish's name. Slurping them up is nothing short of heavenly. In our doggy version, rice is cooked directly in the meatballs to keep them soft. To help balance the dish, we "season" the broth with sea kelp, eggshell, and oysters. Make sure to serve the broth to your pup, too, as it's an essential part of the experience and the nutrition.

1 lb (454 g) lean ground pork or turkey

2 large eggs

2 tbsp (17 g) roasted, unsalted sunflower seeds

1 tbsp (9 g) oyster powder

¾ tsp (5 g) ground eggshell

½ tsp (1 g) sea kelp powder

¼ cup (50 g) uncooked rice, washed

2 tbsp (30 g) olive oil (see note)

2 cups (480 ml) water or dog-friendly broth

4 heads (14 oz / 400 g) baby bok choy, roughly chopped

1. Combine all the ingredients except the water and bok choy in a large bowl. Mix until well incorporated.

2. Form the mixture into meatballs. Traditionally, these are large, fist-sized meatballs. You can make them whatever shape and size will work best for your dog.

3. Bring the water or broth to a boil in a pot over medium heat. Drop the meatballs in, cover the pot, reduce the heat to low, and simmer for 30 minutes, or until they are cooked through. Check the pot periodically to make sure there's enough water. Add another 1 cup (240 ml) of water if needed. Note that it may take a while for the rice to soften all the way through if you made the meatballs large.

4. Add the bok choy in the last 5–6 minutes of cooking.

5. Let the soup cool slightly before portioning into servings for your dog. Cool completely before serving. Store any leftover portions in airtight containers in the fridge for up to 4 days.

Note: If using a fattier blend of ground meat, omit the extra olive oil.

Ciopuppino

GRAIN-FREE, HYPOALLERGENIC 🐾 **MAKES 1,050 CALORIES**

This Italian fish stew is traditionally tomato based, but our doggy-style version is made with pumpkin puree instead. Of course, we still use all the wonderful seafood that gives it both nutrients and umami flavor. If you want this recipe to look just like the human version, you can add a pinch of beet powder (or a handful of chopped fresh beets) to turn this sauce a beautiful bright red.

1 (15 oz / 425 g) can plain pumpkin puree

1 cup (240 ml) water or dog-friendly fish broth

½ tsp (3 g) ground eggshell

½ tsp (1 g) sea kelp powder

Handful of chopped beets or pinch of beet powder (optional)

¼ lb (114 g) fresh or frozen oysters

½ lb (227 g) peeled shrimp

¼ lb (114 g) salmon

3–4 fresh mussels (optional)

3 tbsp (45 g) olive oil

Fresh basil or cilantro (optional)

1. Combine the pumpkin puree and water or broth in a medium pot and bring to a simmer over medium heat. Sprinkle in the ground eggshell and sea kelp powder. Optionally, stir in the chopped beets or beet powder.

2. Add the oysters, shrimp, salmon, and mussels (if using) and cook for 5–8 minutes, or until the seafood is just done.

3. Remove from the heat and stir in the olive oil.

4. If you cooked any seafood with the shells on, remove the shells before serving. Let the stew cool slightly before portioning into servings for your dog. Cool completely before serving. Optionally, top with fresh herbs. Store any leftover portions in airtight containers in the fridge for up to 3 days.

Big Breakfast Skillet

GRAIN-FREE 🐾 **MAKES 2,650 CALORIES**

This recipe is inspired by Southwest breakfast bowls, and it would be the perfect way to energize your dog for a long day of hard work guarding your house (aka barking at the wind). We call it breakfast, but we're sure your pup would enjoy this hearty dish of veggies, beef, and eggs for dinner, too!

2 cups (480 ml) water

½ tsp (1 g) sea kelp powder

2 tbsp (17 g) oyster powder

1 tsp (6 g) ground eggshell

½ small (4 oz / 120 g) sweet potato, cubed

1 cup (80 g) button mushrooms, quartered

1 medium (5 oz / 150 g) zucchini, cubed

1 (15 oz / 425 g) can unsalted black beans, drained

¼ oz (7.5 g) freeze-dried beef liver

1 lb (454 g) 90% lean ground beef

1 (4¼ oz / 125 g) tin unsalted sardines in water, drained

4 large eggs

3 tbsp (26 g) roasted, unsalted sunflower seeds

3 tbsp (45 g) extra-virgin olive oil

1. In your largest saucepan or skillet, bring the water to a boil over medium heat. Stir in the sea kelp powder, oyster powder, and ground eggshell.

2. Add the sweet potato, mushrooms, and zucchini and cook until the sweet potato begins to soften, 8–10 minutes.

3. Add the black beans and beef liver.

4. Add the ground beef in small clumps or balls, wedging them in gaps between the veggies. Add the sardines the same way. Cook until the ground beef is nearly cooked through, about 5 minutes.

5. Make four wells in the mixture and crack an egg into each. If the pan is getting dry, add more water to help steam the eggs.

6. Sprinkle the sunflower seeds in and cover with a lid. Let the eggs cook until just set, with the yolks runny, about 3 minutes.

7. Remove from the heat and let cool completely. Drizzle the olive oil on top just before portioning and serving. Store any leftover portions in airtight containers in the fridge for up to 4 days.

Supermeals

Supermeals are like the Lambarkghinis of the dog food world: thoughtfully crafted with elevated ingredients and balanced to better than AAFCO standards, these meals are formulated to provide your best friend a diverse set of plant and animal compounds that will help them thrive. Our Supermeals call for nutritious plant ingredients like wheat germ and lentils, while also expanding your pup's palate with new proteins like duck, shrimp, and venison. They can be fed every day, but serving them once in a while is more than enough to enhance your pup's diet with variety. They also serve as examples to show the wide range of dog-friendly ingredients out there and inspire your own creations. Note that game meats like bison, venison, and skinless duck are very lean, so we call for additional oil to balance the macronutrients.

These meals are a bit more involved and may include up to 13 ingredients. They also may take more time to prepare, but ultimately you can simplify the recipes by just combining all the ingredients and simmering them together in a pot. That is, if your dog doesn't mind the lack of flair! Cedric and Edith love Seafood Pawella and Lapawgna, and E never complains even when the Lapawgna is less than exquisitely layered.

One-Pan Chicken Bake

MAKES 1,400 CALORIES

There's nothing simpler than throwing all your ingredients onto one baking sheet and straight into the oven. This delicious one-pan bake comes together with little effort and our doggie taste testers rate it four paws up.

¼ oz (7.5 g) freeze-dried beef liver

1 lb (454 g) boneless, skinless chicken thighs (if using chicken skin, omit the extra olive oil)

2 oz (60 g) salmon

1 small (8.5 oz / 240 g) sweet potato, diced

2 medium (120 g) carrots, diced

A few sprigs of rosemary (optional)

¼ cup (30 g) wheat germ (see note)

½ cup (120 ml) water (plus more to rehydrate the liver)

1 tbsp (9 g) oyster powder

¾ tsp (5 g) ground eggshell

½ tsp (1 g) sea kelp powder

2 tbsp (30 g) olive oil

1. Preheat the oven to 375°F (190°C).

2. Rehydrate the freeze-dried liver in a bowl of warm water while the oven preheats.

3. Arrange the chicken, liver, salmon, sweet potato, carrots, and rosemary (if using) on a baking sheet lined with parchment paper.

4. Sprinkle the wheat germ over everything. Pour the ½ cup (120 ml) water into the pan.

5. Bake for 30 minutes, or until the carrots and sweet potato are fork-tender and chicken has reached an internal temperature of 165°F (74°C).

6. Remove from the oven, discard rosemary sprigs (if using), then sprinkle on the oyster powder, ground eggshell, and sea kelp powder. Drizzle on the olive oil.

7. Using two forks, shred the chicken and salmon, and toss everything together to evenly mix. Let the mixture cool slightly before portioning into servings for your dog. Cool completely before serving. Store any leftover portions in airtight containers in the fridge for up to 4 days.

Note: Grains get undeserved criticism—they are a great part of a pup's diet. Wheat germ, in particular, is an underrated and super nutritious option: it contains protein and minerals, and it is a great source of vitamin E.

Venison and Mushroom Farro Risotto

MAKES 1,550 CALORIES

This mushroom dish is for dogs with refined pawlates. We love feeding the dogs novel proteins like venison once in a while to add variety and new flavors to their food. For dogs who are allergic to common proteins like chicken or beef, the dish is a great everyday option. This risotto is made with farro, an ancient grain. Unlike rice-based risottos, it comes together without needing constant stirring.

1 lb (454 g) ground venison

½ oz (15 g) freeze-dried bison liver

1 cup (135 g) frozen peas and carrots

1 cup (100 g) button mushrooms, thinly sliced

1 sprig rosemary

2 oz (60 g) salmon, chopped into bite-sized pieces

½ cup (100 g) farro

2 cups (480 ml) water or dog-friendly bone broth

3 tbsp (45 g) olive oil

1 tbsp (9 g) oyster powder or 3 oz (90 g) fresh or frozen oysters

¾ tsp (5 g) ground eggshell

½ tsp (1 g) sea kelp powder

1. In a large pan over medium heat, cook the ground venison and liver together for a few minutes to brown, breaking the meat up with a spoon. Add the peas and carrots, mushrooms, rosemary sprig, and salmon. Cook for 2 minutes.

2. Add the farro and water or broth to the pan. Bring to a low boil, cover the pan, reduce the heat to low, and simmer for 15–20 minutes, or until the farro expands and fully cooks. Add ½ cup (120 ml) more water if the pan gets dry.

3. Add the olive oil, oyster powder, ground eggshell, and sea kelp powder and stir to combine.

4. Let the risotto cool slightly and discard the rosemary sprig before portioning into servings for your dog. Cool completely before serving. Store any leftover portions in airtight containers in the fridge for up to 4 days.

Note: May we suggest a glass of Pupnot Noir (page 285) to go with this risotto?

Note: If your dog is sensitive to wheat, substitute the farro for wild rice, rolled oats, or quinoa.

Turkey Meatballs and Hummus

MAKES 3,300 CALORIES

Hummus, the widely beloved chickpea dish that originated in the Middle East, is surprisingly great for dogs, too. We serve the hummus as a side for these juicy homemade meatballs to make a complete meal. This is a big batch, so if you're making the dish for a smaller dog, freeze what can't be consumed in 4 days. To make it grain-free, omit the wheat germ.

Meatballs

2 lb (908 g) lean ground turkey

7 oz (200 g) chicken liver, minced

5 tbsp (45 g) roasted, unsalted sunflower seeds

1 cup (120 g) finely chopped broccoli

1 cup (100 g) finely chopped spinach

1 (4¼ oz / 125 g) tin unsalted sardines in water, drained

Hummus

1 (14½ oz / 400 g) can unsalted chickpeas, drained and rinsed

3 tbsp (45 g) olive oil

2 tbsp (17 g) oyster powder

1¼ tsp (7½ g) ground eggshell

1 tsp (2 g) sea kelp powder

¼ cup (60 ml) water (or as needed)

To Serve

1 cup (150 g) chopped cucumber

Fresh basil or mint leaves (optional)

Sprinkle of wheat germ (optional)

Meatballs

1. Preheat the oven to 350°F (175°C).

2. In a large bowl or a food processor, combine the ground turkey, liver, sunflower seeds, broccoli, spinach, and sardines.

3. Form the mixture into little meatballs and arrange them on a baking sheet.

4. Bake for 25 minutes, or until the meatballs are cooked through and the internal temperature reaches 165°F (75°C).

Hummus

1. Meanwhile, in a blender or food processor, combine the chickpeas, olive oil, oyster powder, ground eggshell, and sea kelp powder. Pulse until you have a smooth paste. Add the water in small splashes as needed to help the mixture blend smoothly.

2. Let the meatballs cool slightly before portioning the hummus and meatballs into servings for your dog. Cool completely before serving. Top with the cucumber and sprinkle with wheat germ (if using), fresh mint, or basil (if using). Store any leftover portions in airtight containers in the fridge for up to 4 days, or freeze for up to 6 months.

Gumbark

HYPOALLERGENIC 🐾 **MAKES 1,900 CALORIES**

Gumbo, famous in Louisiana and with West African origins, is a meat and seafood stew full of flavor and nutrients. Instead of using ground pork, which is usually a fattier blend, this recipe calls for chopped lean pork. The aroma is enough to excite any dog, and the best part is that our Gumbark uses pork and seafood—great alternatives for dogs with sensitivities to common proteins.

½ lb (227 g) lean boneless pork chop, minced

¼ lb (114 g) salmon

2 cups (270 g) frozen peas and carrots

½ oz (15 g) freeze-dried pork or bison liver chunks

2 tbsp (17 g) roasted, unsalted sunflower seeds

⅛ cup (25 g) uncooked rice, washed

3 tbsp (45 g) olive oil

2 tbsp (17 g) oyster powder

¾ tsp (5 g) ground eggshell

½ tsp (1 g) sea kelp powder

2 cups (480 ml) water or dog-friendly bone broth

½ lb (227 g) fresh or frozen shrimp, optionally chopped

Handful of cilantro, for garnish (optional)

1. Combine all the ingredients except the shrimp and cilantro in a pot and bring to a boil on medium heat. Turn the heat down to low and simmer for 15 minutes, or until the minced pork chop and salmon are cooked, or until the rice is tender.

2. Add the shrimp and cook for 3–5 minutes, or until they turn opaque and curl into a C shape.

3. Remove from the heat. Let the stew cool slightly before portioning into servings for your dog. Cool before serving and garnish with cilantro (if using). Store any leftover portions in airtight containers in the fridge for up to 4 days.

Lamb and Lentil Curry

MAKES 2,500 CALORIES

Lentils are a great addition to any canine diet. They are high in soluble fiber and also have a decent amount of plant protein. This curry uses lamb, turmeric, and yogurt to create a fragrant meal that will delight your pup's senses.

1 (15 oz / 425 g) can plain pumpkin puree

1 lb (454 g) lean lamb stew meat, chopped into bite-sized pieces

1 oz (30 g) freeze-dried or 3½ oz (100 g) fresh beef heart, chopped

3½ oz (100 g) salmon

1 medium head (9 oz / 260 g) broccoli, roughly chopped

2 medium (4 oz / 120 g) carrots, roughly chopped

3½ oz (100 g) dry red lentils

Pinch of ground turmeric or grated fresh turmeric

2 tbsp (17 g) roasted, unsalted sunflower seeds

2 tbsp (30 g) olive oil

2 tbsp (17 g) oyster powder

1 tsp (6 g) ground eggshell

½ tsp (1 g) sea kelp powder

1 cup (240 ml) water or dog-friendly bone broth

1 cup (240 ml) full-fat plain yogurt or plain coconut yogurt

1. Combine all the ingredients except the yogurt in a pot on medium heat. Bring to a boil, reduce the heat to low, and simmer for 15–20 minutes, or until the lentils are tender.

2. Remove from the heat and stir in the yogurt. Let the curry cool slightly before portioning into servings for your dog. Cool completely before serving. Store any leftover portions in airtight containers in the fridge for up to 4 days.

Pineapup Fried Rice

MAKES 2,400 CALORIES

This fried rice has a special ingredient—pineapple!

Pineapple fried rice is a Thai-inspired dish that our dogs *love* for its combo of meat, juicy fruit, and eggs. Snack on some fresh pineapple with your dog as you're cooking for a nice vitamin-packed treat. Serving the dish inside a pineapple "bowl" is completely optional. If you do, just make sure your dog doesn't eat the leafy top, core, or rind.

½ cup (95 g) uncooked rice, washed

1 lb (454 g) lean ground beef

⅓ oz (9 g) freeze-dried beef liver

2 oz (60 g) salmon, chopped into bite-sized pieces

4 large eggs

2 heads (7 oz / 200 g) baby bok choy, roughly chopped

¼ cup (30 g) wheat germ

1 tbsp (9 g) oyster powder

¾ tsp (5 g) ground eggshell

½ tsp (1 g) sea kelp powder

Pinch of ground turmeric

1 cup (160 g) fresh pineapple chunks

2 tbsp (30 g) olive oil

1. Cook the rice in a rice cooker or on the stove according to the package directions.

2. Heat a wok on medium heat. Add a splash of water. Cook the beef, beef liver, and salmon, stirring occasionally, for 5 minutes, or until the beef is browned.

3. Scoot the meat to the side of the wok (or temporarily transfer it to a bowl if your wok isn't large enough). Crack in the eggs and scramble lightly.

4. Add the bok choy, wheat germ, cooked rice, oyster powder, ground eggshell, sea kelp powder, and turmeric. Toss everything together. Cook for an additional 5 minutes, or until the bok choy is softened.

5. Remove the wok from the heat and stir in the pineapple chunks and olive oil.

6. Let the fried rice cool slightly before portioning into servings for your dog. Cool completely before serving. Store any leftover portions in airtight containers in the fridge for up to 3 days.

Venison Bourdognon

GRAIN-FREE 🐾 **MAKES 1,425 CALORIES**

This play on the famous bourguignon calls for venison meat, though you could also use beef (if using beef, reduce the olive oil by half). Our version stays as true to the real thing as we can, with mushrooms and carrots, and just a few changes to make it good for your dog. We'd like to think Julia Child would have approved!

1 lb (454 g) ground venison or venison stew chunks

¼ oz (7.5 g) freeze-dried beef liver

1 cup (120 g) cubed carrots

1 cup (130 g) cubed beets

1 cup (80 g) button mushrooms, quartered

1 (4¼ oz / 125 g) tin unsalted sardines in water, drained

1 cup (50 g) chopped kale

1 tbsp (9 g) oyster powder

1 tsp (5 g) ground eggshell

½ tsp (1 g) sea kelp powder

4 tbsp (60 g) olive oil*

1. Combine the venison, beef liver, carrots, beets, and mushrooms in a Dutch oven and cover with water. Bring to a boil over medium heat. Once the mixture is boiling, reduce the heat to low, cover with a lid, and simmer for at least 1 hour. The longer you stew the meat, the more tender it will become.

2. When everything is nicely stewed, stir in the sardines, kale, oyster powder, ground eggshell, and sea kelp powder.

3. Remove from the heat and drizzle in the olive oil. Let the stew cool slightly before portioning into servings for your dog. Cool completely before serving. Store any leftover portions in airtight containers in the fridge for up to 4 days.

*As venison is so lean, we add extra olive oil as a source of healthy fat.

Lapawgna

MAKES 2,200 CALORIES WITHOUT CHEESE

Lasagna has to be the dreamiest pasta dish. The layers of meat, cheese, sauce, and noodles are a rare treat for us, as it's a bit of an effort to make. The dogs get Lapawgna more often than we get lasagna! To save time on this recipe, you can use store-bought lasagna sheets. Many stores supply a variety of rice- and lentil-based options, too, if your dog is sensitive to wheat. Cheese is optional but Cedric highly recommends adding it.

Lasagna Sheets

2 large eggs

1 cup (100 g) oat flour or chickpea flour, plus more as needed and for rolling

Meat Filling

1 lb (454 g) lean ground bison

1 (15 oz / 425 g) can plain pumpkin puree

Pinch of beet powder or handful of chopped fresh beets (optional)

1 (4¼ oz / 125 g) tin unsalted sardines in water, drained

3 tbsp (45 g) olive oil

1 tbsp (9 g) oyster powder

1½ tsp (7.5 g) ground eggshell

½ tsp (1 g) sea kelp powder

⅓ cup (40 g) wheat germ (save 1 tbsp / 6 g for sprinkling on top)

Topping

Shredded mozzarella cheese (optional)

For a low-carb Lapawgna, swap the noodles for thinly sliced zucchini or squash.

1. Preheat the oven to 350°F (175°C).

Lasagna Sheets

1. In a bowl, combine the eggs with the flour until a soft dough forms. You may need to add more flour if it's too wet, or a splash of water if it's too dry.

2. Roll the dough out on a floured surface until it's quite thin (think regular lasagna sheets). Slice into rectangles that will fit into your casserole dish.

Assembly

1. Stir together all the filling ingredients in a mixing bowl (the filling goes in raw and will cook in the oven).

2. Spoon a layer of the filling into an 8-inch (20-cm) square casserole dish, cover with a layer of noodle sheets, and repeat, finishing with a layer of filling on top.

3. Sprinkle on top a layer of shredded mozzarella cheese (if using) and 1 tbsp (6 g) wheat germ.

4. Bake for 1 hour, or until bubbling and golden brown. Let the Lapawgna cool slightly before portioning into servings for your dog. Cool completely before serving. Store leftover portions in airtight containers in the fridge for up to 4 days.

Steamed Egg with Minced Pork

MAKES 950 CALORIES WITHOUT RICE, 1,050 CALORIES WITH RICE

This dish is a pup-friendly version of another one of our childhood comfort foods. Though we would normally eat this with rice on the side, we opt to steam it directly into the dish for convenience. You can omit rice to make this lower-carb.

¼ lb (114 g) finely minced lean pork chops or lean ground pork

2 oz (60 g) salmon, minced

1 medium (2 oz / 60 g) carrot, grated or finely chopped

½ small (4 oz / 120 g) sweet potato, grated or finely chopped

1 head (3.5 oz / 100 g) baby bok choy, finely chopped

2 tbsp (12 g) wheat germ

¼ cup (50 g) uncooked rice, washed (optional)

3 large eggs

½ cup (120 ml) water or dog-friendly bone broth

½ tbsp (4 g) oyster powder

½ tsp (3 g) ground eggshell

½ tsp (1 g) sea kelp powder

1 tbsp (15 g) olive oil

1. Fill a steamer pot with water and bring to a boil over medium-high heat.

2. In a mixing bowl, thoroughly combine the pork, salmon, carrot, sweet potato, bok choy, wheat germ, and rice (if using).

3. Press the mixture into the bottom of 1-quart (1-liter) heat-safe dish. Transfer the dish to the steamer and steam over a rolling boil for 10 minutes, until the meat is fully cooked, or for 18 minutes if you used rice.

4. Meanwhile, in a bowl, whisk the eggs with the water or broth, oyster powder, ground eggshell, and sea kelp powder. Pour the egg mixture on top of the meat and steam for 7–8 more minutes on a low simmer, or until the egg has just set but is still jiggly.

5. Let the food cool slightly and drizzle with olive oil before portioning into servings for your dog. Cool completely before serving. Store any leftover portions in airtight containers in the fridge for up to 4 days.

Japanese Dogsu Curry

MAKES 1,670 CALORIES

This dish is our take on a Japanese katsu (dogsu, get it?) curry, which is typically a rich but mild curry served over a breaded chicken or pork cutlet.

Breaded Cutlet

½ cup (45 g) rolled oats

1 large egg

1 lb (454 g) lean chicken breast or pork chop (about 2 pieces)

Curry

1 (15 oz / 425 g) can plain pumpkin puree

½ cup (120 ml) water

1 medium (2 oz / 60 g) carrot, roughly chopped

2 oz (60 g) salmon, chopped into bite-sized pieces

1 tbsp (9 g) roasted, unsalted sunflower seeds

1 tbsp (9 g) oyster powder

¾ tsp (5 g) ground eggshell

½ tsp (1 g) sea kelp powder

1 tsp (2g) grated ginger (optional)

½ tsp (1.5 g) turmeric (optional)

1 tbsp (15 g) olive oil

Sprig of cilantro (optional)

1. Preheat the oven to 375°F (190°C). Line a rimmed baking sheet with parchment paper.

2. Pulse the rolled oats in a blender 1–2 times until they are slightly broken down, but don't turn them into flour.

3. Transfer the oats to a bowl and whisk them together with the egg.

4. Coat the chicken or pork chops in the egg and oat mixture. Then transfer them to the baking sheet.

5. Bake for 25–30 minutes, or until the internal temperature reaches 165°F (74°C).

6. Meanwhile, to make the curry, combine all of the curry ingredients except for the olive oil and cilantro in a large pot and bring to a simmer on medium-low. Cook for 15–20 minutes or until the carrots have softened. Remove from heat and stir in the olive oil.

7. Let the cutlet rest for 5–10 minutes before slicing into thin pieces.

8. Plate the cutlet with the curry and garnish with cilantro (if using). Cool completely before serving. Store any leftover portions in airtight containers in the fridge for up to 4 days.

> Quick version: To skip the breaded cutlet, chop the meat into bite-sized pieces. Add the meat, egg, and rolled oats directly to the curry to cook.

Dogle Pie

MAKES 2,600 CALORIES

Lamb is a great protein alternative for dogs allergic to beef or chicken. This flavorful lamb pie, modeled after the Irish specialty Dingle pie, has a unique coconut flour crust that resembles corn bread and stays soft after baking.

Filling

1 lb (454 g) lean lamb stew meat

2 cups (240 g) diced carrots

⅓ oz (9 g) freeze-dried beef liver

1 cup water (or as needed)

1 small sprig rosemary (optional)

1 (4¼ oz / 125 g) tin unsalted sardines in water, drained

1 cup (100 g) chopped spinach

½ cup (60 g) wheat germ

1 tbsp (9 g) oyster powder

1½ tsp (7.5 g) ground eggshell

½ tsp (1 g) sea kelp powder

1 tsp (3 g) carob powder (optional)

2 tsp (6 g) coconut flour

Crust

1 cup (100 g) coconut flour

2 large eggs

3 tbsp (45 g) olive oil

1. Preheat the oven to 375°F (190°C).

2. In a large pot, add the lamb, carrots, liver, and water. Bring to a boil on medium-high heat, then reduce the heat to low and simmer for 10 minutes. Add the rosemary sprig (if using).

3. Add the sardines, spinach, wheat germ, oyster powder, ground eggshell, sea kelp powder, and carob powder (if using).

4. Remove the rosemary sprig (if using). Stir in the 2 tsp (6 g) coconut flour to thicken the sauce to a gravy consistency. Remove from the heat.

5. In a separate bowl, mix the 1 cup (100 g) coconut flour, eggs, and olive oil to make the crust batter. It will be thick, with the texture of a fluffy cookie dough. If you find it to be too dry and crumbly, add a splash of water.

6. Transfer the meat mixture to an 8-inch (20-cm) round baking dish, then spread the batter over the top, pressing it down into an even layer as you go.

7. Bake for 25–35 minutes, or until the crust is set and golden brown.

8. Let the pie cool slightly before portioning into servings for your dog. Cool completely before serving. Store any leftover portions in airtight containers in the fridge for up to 4 days.

Tuscan Bean Stew

HYPOALLERGENIC ☙ **MAKES 2,250 CALORIES**

This comfort dish combines beans with lamb, a novel protein, plus fresh spinach and carrots.

1 lb (454 g) lean ground lamb or cubed stew meat

1 (15 oz / 425 g) can unsalted navy beans, drained

2 (4¼ oz / 125 g) tins unsalted sardines in water, drained

1 oz (30 g) freeze-dried lamb or bison liver

2 medium (4 oz / 120 g) carrots, roughly chopped

½ cup (50 g) chopped spinach

¼ cup (45 g) dry quinoa

1 tbsp (9 g) roasted, unsalted sunflower seeds

1 tbsp (15 g) olive oil

1 tbsp (9 g) oyster powder

¾ tsp (5 g) ground eggshell

½ tsp (1 g) sea kelp powder

2 cups (480 ml) water or dog-friendly bone broth

1. Combine all the ingredients in a pot. Bring to a boil on medium heat, reduce the heat to low, and cover with a lid. Simmer, stirring occasionally to ensure even cooking, for 20–25 minutes.

2. Let the stew cool slightly before portioning into servings for your dog. Cool completely before serving. Store any leftover portions in airtight containers in the fridge for up to 4 days.

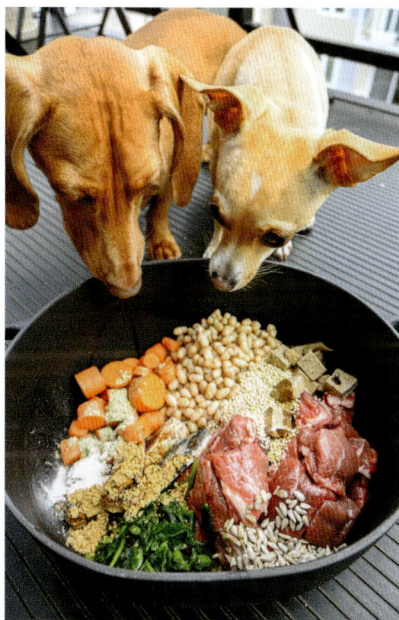

If you prefer to use dried beans, follow the package instructions for soaking and thoroughly cooking them before you use them in a recipe. Never add dry beans directly to a recipe.

Seafood Pawella

MAKES 1,675 CALORIES

Seafood is so nutritious. It's packed with vitamins, minerals, and amazing omega-3s. Making it a part of your dog's varied diet will not only benefit their health but also bring them lots of enjoyment. The aromas from this dish bubbling away on your stove will have everyone in the house drooling and pulling out all their tricks for a bite.

3 tbsp (45 g) olive oil

½ lb (227 g) ground chicken

1¾ oz (50 g) chicken liver, minced

1 cup (80 g) maitake mushrooms, finely chopped

¼ lb (114 g) salmon, chopped into bite-sized pieces

½ cup (95 g) uncooked rice, washed

2 tbsp (17 g) oyster powder

¾ tsp (5 g) ground eggshell

½ tsp (1 g) sea kelp powder

1 tsp (3 g) ground turmeric (optional)

2 cups (480 ml) water or dog-friendly bone broth

½ cup (75 g) frozen peas

¼ lb (114 g) peeled shrimp

1. In a large saucepan with a lid, cook the olive oil, ground chicken, chicken liver, and mushrooms over medium heat for about 5 minutes, breaking up the meat with a spoon.

2. Stir in the salmon, rice, oyster powder, ground eggshell, sea kelp powder, turmeric, and water or broth. Bring to a boil, reduce the heat to low, cover with the lid, and simmer for 12 minutes. If the pan is dry, add ½ cup (120 ml) more water.

3. Add the peas and shrimp, and cover with the lid again, allowing everything to steam for 5–6 more minutes, or until the shrimp are opaque and the rice is tender.

4. Let the Pawella cool slightly before portioning into servings for your dog. Cool completely before serving. Store any leftover portions in airtight containers in the fridge for up to 4 days.

Thai Green Curry

MAKES 2,100 CALORIES

Thai cuisine is one of our favorites, and in Thai green curry, the sweet, fragrant, and herbaceous flavors come together perfectly. While Thai green curry paste is often made with green chilies, garlic, and shallot (among other ingredients), our dog-friendly version gets its vibrant color from broccoli.

Rice
½ cup (95 g) uncooked wild rice, washed (optional)

Curry Paste
1 medium head (9 oz / 260 g) broccoli or 2 cups frozen florets

1 small slice (½ oz / 20 g) ginger

2 tbsp (30 g) olive oil

1 tbsp (9 g) oyster powder

¾ tsp (5 g) ground eggshell

½ tsp (1 g) sea kelp powder

1–2 Thai basil leaves (optional)

Curry
1 lb (454 g) boneless, skinless chicken thighs, chopped

3½ oz (100 g) fresh chicken liver, chopped

½ cup (120 ml) water or dog-friendly broth

½ cup (60 g) thinly sliced mushrooms, zucchini, red bell pepper, and/or bamboo shoots (optional)

1 (4¼ oz / 125 g) tin unsalted sardines in water, drained

¼ cup (30 g) wheat germ

1 cup (240 ml) coconut milk or plain coconut yogurt

1. If serving with rice, cook the rice according to the package directions.

2. In a food processor, combine the curry paste ingredients and pulse until you have a rough, thick paste.

3. Heat a pan on low. Cook the curry paste for 3–5 minutes, or until fragrant.

4. Add the chicken thighs and liver. Cover with the water or broth and bring to a bubble. Optionally, add the mushrooms, zucchini, red bell pepper, and bamboo shoots. Cover the pan and simmer for 8–10 minutes, or until the chicken is cooked through. If you added mushrooms, make sure they are thoroughly cooked as well.

5. Add the sardines and wheat germ.

6. Remove from the heat. Stir in the coconut milk or yogurt.

7. Stir in the cooked rice (or serve rice on the side). Let the curry cool slightly before portioning into servings for your dog. Cool completely before serving. Store any leftover portions in airtight containers in the fridge for up to 4 days.

Duck à l'Orpawnge

GRAIN-FREE ❧ **HYPOALLERGENIC** ❧ **MAKES 560 CALORIES**

Duck is a great novel protein with so much flavor. This stunning dish inspired by the French classic is fit to be served at any Michelin-pawed restaurant.

1 tbsp (15 g) olive oil

1 sprig rosemary (optional)

1 (5 oz / 150 g) duck breast, skin removed

½ cup (2 oz / 60 g) chopped carrots

½ cup (60 g) chopped sweet potato

1 oz (30 g) salmon

1 tbsp (9 g) oyster powder

¼ tsp (1½ g) ground eggshell

¼ tsp (½ g) sea kelp powder

1–3 orange segments, for plating

1. Heat the olive oil in a pan over medium heat. Add the rosemary to the pan to infuse flavor. When rosemary is sizzling, add the duck breast and sear for 4–5 minutes on each side. Transfer the duck to a plate. Discard the rosemary sprig.

2. In the same pan, add the carrots and sweet potato. Cover with water and bring to a boil. Reduce the heat to low and simmer for 10 minutes, or until the sweet potato is fork-tender.

3. Add the salmon and poach for 2–3 minutes.

4. Transfer the carrots, sweet potato, and salmon to a blender.

5. Add the oyster powder, ground eggshell, sea kelp powder, and a splash of water to the blender. Pulse until you have a puree. Add more water if needed.

6. Slice the duck and plate with the puree and orange segments. Cool completely before portioning and serving. Store any leftover portions in airtight containers in the fridge for up to 4 days.

Barkers and Mash

MAKES 1,800 CALORIES

In the United Kingdom, "bangers" is a playful term for sausages. The name actually comes from World War I when sausages had a high water content, causing them to explode when cooked. For Cedric and Edith, these sausages are called Barkers because they are so good, they make them bark!

1 lb (454 g) 90% lean ground chicken

3½ oz (100 g) chicken liver, chopped

1 (4¼ oz / 125 g) tin unsalted sardines in water, drained

¼ cup (30 g) wheat germ

1 tbsp (9 g) oyster powder

½ tsp (1 g) sea kelp powder

½ tsp (1.5 g) carob powder

½ cup (120 ml) water

1 tsp (2 g) psyllium husk or oat flour

1 small (8.5 oz / 240 g) sweet potato, peeled and cubed

1 cup (150 g) frozen peas

1. In a large bowl, combine the ground chicken, chicken liver, sardines, and wheat germ. Form the mixture into sausages of your preferred size.

2. Heat a pan over medium heat. Place the sausages in the pan with a splash of water. Cover with a lid and steam until cooked through (when the internal temperature reaches 165°F / 74°C). Transfer the sausages to a plate.

3. In the same pan, add the oyster powder, sea kelp powder, carob powder, and water. Bring to a bubble and stir in the psyllium husk or oat flour. Allow a few minutes for the gravy to thicken. Remove from the heat.

4. Bring a pot of water to a boil over medium-high heat and add the sweet potato. Cook for 8–10 minutes, or until fork-tender.

5. Transfer the sweet potato to a bowl and mash with a fork.

6. To the same hot water, add the peas and boil for 3–5 minutes, or until soft.

7. Let everything cool slightly before portioning into servings for your dog; plate some sausages alongside the mash and peas and top with gravy. Cool completely before serving. Store any leftover portions in airtight containers in the fridge for up to 4 days.

Special Diets

Your dog is never too young or too old to enjoy real food! Just like people's dietary needs change in different stages of life, so too do dogs' dietary needs. For example, puppies and senior dogs need more protein than what you'd regularly feed adult dogs. In "Special Diets," you'll find recipes created for puppies and their mommas, for senior dogs over 10 (depending on the breed), for athletes and working dogs, and for weight loss.

Puppies and Mothers

The arrival of new puppies is a joyful occasion. What better way to celebrate and show them your love than with real food?

Both mom and puppies have special nutritional needs during this life stage (that is, when the pups need more calories than Momma's milk can provide and are ready for solid food, at about four weeks old).

For puppies, expectant mothers, and nursing mothers, AAFCO provides the same guidelines, termed "Growth and Reproduction." However, this is a case where we think AAFCO's guidelines aren't nuanced enough to cover dogs' different needs. There are many differences just between different dog breeds, let alone expectant mothers during different periods of gestation. Lactating mothers also have slightly different dietary needs. Of particular concern is the lack of guidelines for omega-3 fatty acid consumption, which is essential for optimal neurological development for all phases of growth and reproduction.

Here's a brief overview of how dogs' needs shift during pregnancy, lactation, and growth.

Mommas

In dogs, pregnancy normally lasts between 57 and 65 days. AAFCO Growth and Reproduction guidelines dictate higher sodium intake during gestation. But in the earliest part of a dog's pregnancy (before about week three), she doesn't need that much sodium quite yet. Peak sodium requirements start around week five, when fetal development accelerates and she needs to produce more amniotic fluid. A maintenance diet with added omega-3s, micronutrients, and bonemeal instead of eggshell (rather than a special reproductive diet) is more appropriate for the first few weeks of gestation.

As gestation progresses and a dog reaches mid to late term, her nutritional requirements ramp up quickly, especially in the last several weeks. Depending on the size of her litter, she could need up to 150 percent or more of her normal caloric intake. She'll need more fat and protein because these serve as cellular building blocks. The bone-building minerals calcium and phosphorus are needed for fast growth of the pups. Her sodium requirements peak in the third trimester, but this should be met carefully as the expectant mother's rapid weight gain puts stress on her kidneys and liver. Offer her plenty of water, and as always, feed fish, fish oil, or krill oil for omega-3s EPA and DHA to ensure proper development of puppy brains and eyes. Krill oil is both more stable and more bioavailable than fish oil; 1–2 grams of either per day is easily tolerated.

After birth, lactating mothers expend lots of energy producing milk. Depending on the size of her litter, she could need 200–300 percent of her normal caloric intake, or more. The bone-building minerals calcium and phosphorus are needed for fast growth of the pups just as during later stages of gestation.

Puppies

Puppies need extra calcium and phosphorus to help their bones grow. Once a puppy reaches their expected height or about 80 percent of their adult weight, switch from growth formulas to adult recipes; the extra minerals in puppy recipes can put unnecessary strain on dogs' kidneys. Of course, the age at which a dog reaches their maximum height depends a lot on their breed.

Because small-breed puppies need to put on less bone mass and grow for a shorter period of time, they should be fed growth formulas for a shorter time. By six to eight months of age, small-breed dogs should be fully grown and switched to Adult Maintenance Recipes.

Medium-sized breeds can be kept on growth formulas for up to about one year.

Some large-breed puppies reach adult height at around two years of age and continue to put on weight for months after. Once a dog's maximum height is reached, puppy recipes should be switched to adult recipes as the extra minerals are unnecessary.

With these recipes, you can help Momma and babies thrive. Because puppies and mothers have increased calcium and phosphorus requirements, we add bonemeal for most of the recipes. You can find human-grade bonemeal supplements on Amazon or in health-food stores.

Edith, 3 months

Cedric, 2 months

Bison Booster

MAKES 2,100 CALORIES

Formulated especially for young puppies that are growing fast (zero to six months for medium breeds), this meal is also suitable for lactating mothers. Bison is great for growth recipes because it's nutritious and high in protein. Pairing bison with a high-quality complex carb like quinoa makes for a wonderful meal for young pups.

¼ cup (45 g) dry quinoa

1 lb (454 g) ground bison

1 oz (30 g) fresh chicken liver, minced

2 cups (270 g) frozen peas and carrots

1 (4¼ oz / 125 g) tin unsalted sardines in water, drained

⅓ cup (40 g) wheat germ

2½ tbsp (20 g) oyster powder

3 tbsp (27 g) bonemeal

½ tsp (1 g) sea kelp powder

¼ tsp (1 g) sea salt

2 tbsp (30 g) olive oil

1. Cook the quinoa according to the package directions.

2. In a pan on low heat, gently cook the ground bison, chicken liver, and peas and carrots with a splash of water until browned and cooked through, about 8 minutes.

3. Transfer the cooked quinoa, meat, and veggies to a large bowl. Stir in the sardines, wheat germ, oyster powder, bonemeal, sea kelp powder, sea salt, and olive oil.

4. Let the food cool slightly before portioning into servings for your dog. Cool completely before serving. Store any leftover portions in airtight containers in the fridge for up to 4 days.

Puppy Protein Stew

MAKES 2,650 CALORIES

This hearty green stew will nourish the hungriest puppy bellies. This late-growth formulation (six to twelve months for medium-sized dogs) is protein heavy and contains bonemeal for added calcium and phosphorus, but with slightly reduced sodium and iron compared to early-growth formulas. This meal is also suitable for mid-gestation mothers (from about weeks two through four).

1 medium head
(9 oz / 260 g) broccoli,
finely chopped

1 lb (454 g) 90% lean
ground beef

1 lb (454 g) beef heart,
chopped

¼ oz (7.5 g) freeze-dried
beef liver

3½ oz (100 g) salmon

1 cup (90 g) rolled oats

½ cup (60 g) wheat
germ

2 tbsp (17 g) oyster
powder

3 tbsp (27 g) bonemeal

½ tsp (1 g) sea kelp
powder

½ tsp (2 g) table salt

2 cups (480 ml) water

2 tbsp (30 g) olive oil

1. Combine all the ingredients except the olive oil in a pot. Bring to a boil over medium heat, reduce the heat to low, and simmer for 15 minutes, or until the oats are soft.

2. Remove from the heat and stir in the olive oil.

3. Let the food cool slightly before portioning into servings for your dog. Cool completely before serving. Store any leftover portions in airtight containers in the fridge for up to 4 days.

Puppy's First Chowder

MAKES 1,025 CALORIES

Young pups will be sure to devour this comforting seafood chowder. This growth recipe makes a smaller amount of food for small puppies but is still rich in nutrients such as omega-3 fatty acids and protein. It's formulated for prime development and can be fed to lactating moms and puppies in their most critical growth phases.

½ lb (227 g) beef heart, chopped

1 oz (30 g) fresh chicken liver

1 cup (110 g) cauliflower

¼ cup (25 g) rolled oats

1 cup (240 ml) water or dog-friendly broth

¼ lb (114 g) salmon, chopped into small cubes

¼ lb (114 g) shrimp, diced

3 tbsp (12 g) wheat germ

1 tbsp (9 g) oyster powder

4 tsp (12 g) bonemeal

½ tsp (1 g) sea kelp powder

⅛ tsp (0.5 g) sea salt

1 tbsp (15 g) olive oil

1. In a pot, cook the beef heart and chicken liver on medium heat for 6–8 minutes, or until the meat has browned.

2. Add the cauliflower, oats, and broth or water to the pot and bring to a boil. Then reduce the heat to low and simmer for 10 minutes, or until the oats are soft.

3. Add the salmon and shrimp and cook for 5 more minutes, or until the salmon is firm and the shrimp is pink.

4. Add the wheat germ, oyster powder, bonemeal, sea kelp powder, sea salt, and olive oil. Stir and remove from the heat.

5. Let the chowder cool slightly before portioning into servings for your dog. Cool completely before serving. Store any leftover portions in airtight containers in the fridge for up to 4 days.

Momma's Bento Box

MAKES 1,450 CALORIES

Bento boxes have a rich history going back to the sixteenth century in Japan. In a bento box, tiers or compartments keep each component of a meal separate from the others to maintain the distinct flavors. We keep this recipe minimal, with no processing other than gentle steaming, to preserve the moisture and nutrients in each ingredient. Give Momma the culinary experience she deserves, plus the nutrition she needs to feed her pups!

Bento Box Ingredients

¼ lb (114 g) boneless, skinless chicken thighs, chopped into bite-sized pieces

3 oz (90 g) salmon, chopped into bite-sized pieces

2 large eggs

3 oz (90 g) chicken liver

¼ lb (114 g) beef heart, chopped into bite-sized pieces

½ cup (50 g) broccoli florets

½ small (4 oz / 120 g) sweet potato, cubed

3½ oz (100 g) fresh oysters

Toppings

2 tbsp (18 g) bonemeal

¼ cup (30 g) wheat germ

½ tsp (1 g) sea kelp powder

1. Fill a steamer pot with water and bring to a boil over medium heat. Prepare two large bamboo steaming baskets. If you only have one, steam in two batches.

2. Place each bento box ingredient in a small, individual heatproof bowl and arrange in the steamer. Or arrange all the bento box ingredients in one large heatproof bowl that can still fit into your steamer.

3. Sprinkle the bonemeal, wheat germ, and sea kelp powder over the ingredients. We sprinkled the bonemeal and wheat germ onto the chicken, and the sea kelp over the salmon.

4. Steam all the ingredients. After 8–9 minutes, remove the eggs. Continue steaming the rest of the ingredients for another 12–16 minutes, or until the chicken is cooked through. Meanwhile, transfer the eggs to an ice bath and then peel the cooled eggs.

5. Let the food cool before serving. Arrange a small bit of each ingredient on a tray for Momma to explore and eat. You can keep the ingredients separate or mix them all together. Store in airtight containers in the fridge for up to 4 days.

Turkey and Puplings

MAKES 2,400 CALORIES

Inspired by the quintessential southern dish chicken and dumplings, our Turkey and Puplings offers a bowlful of comfort for a momma-to-be. Formulated for pregnant moms early in gestation, this recipe is lower in calcium and phosphorus than growth formulas but has extra omega-3s, a little extra sodium, and extra micronutrients, like zinc, selenium, and manganese, to support early fetal development.

Puplings

1 lb (454 g) 90% lean ground turkey

7 oz (200 g) salmon, minced

3½ oz (100 g) fresh chicken liver, minced

1 large egg

3 tbsp (27 g) bonemeal

½ cup (50 g) oat flour

¼ cup (30 g) wheat germ

Soup

2 cups (480 ml) water or dog-friendly broth

1 cup (135 g) frozen peas and carrots

½ cup (50 g) chopped spinach

Large pinch of oat flour, for thickening (optional)

3 tbsp (27 g) oyster powder

½ tsp (1 g) sea kelp powder

3 tbsp (45 g) olive oil

1. In a bowl, combine the turkey, salmon, liver, egg, bonemeal, oat flour, and wheat germ and mix until thoroughly incorporated.

2. Pour the water or broth into a pot and bring to a boil over medium heat.

3. Using a spoon or your hands, scoop up small balls (approximately 1 inch / 3 cm in diameter) of the meat mixture and drop them into the boiling water. Cook for 5 minutes, or until firm.

4. Add the peas and carrots, spinach, large pinch of oat flour (optional, to thicken), oyster powder, and sea kelp powder. Continue to cook for 6–8 minutes, or until the Puplings have puffed up and the soup has thickened.

5. Remove from the heat and stir in the olive oil.

6. Let the Turkey and Puplings cool slightly before portioning into servings for your dog. Cool completely before serving. Store any leftover portions in airtight containers in the fridge for up to 4 days.

Spaghetti Squash with Bison | 142

Senior Dogs

Caring for aging dogs can be both wonderful and heartbreaking. Seeing dogs transition from active and energetic adults into slower-paced seniors helps put our own lives into perspective. Larger breeds typically slow down after about seven to eight years, while smaller breeds may remain energetic for twelve or more years. However, as we discussed previously, aging can be influenced by a number of factors, including diet and physical activity. Poor diets, overeating, and a lack of activity can lead to unnecessary chronic disease, shorter lifespans, and unnecessary pain for our best friends.

Since AAFCO does not publish feed standards for senior dogs, formulations are made at the discretion of manufacturers and vary widely between brands. Many brands and vets recommend reducing older dogs' protein intake, but science doesn't back this up.[37] Our formulations *increase* protein to prevent sarcopenia, the age-associated loss of muscle mass. Also, because older dogs tend to move less and have insulin insensitivity, these recipes are lower in carbohydrates than typical Adult Maintenance meals.[38] As always, keeping aging dogs lean will help preserve their joints and improve metabolic health in their later years of life. These recipes are also suitable for dogs that are less tolerant of carbohydrates.

Salisbury Steak

MAKES 750 CALORIES, 53% FROM FAT, 37% FROM PROTEIN, 10% FROM CARBOHYDRATE

There's nothing wrong with meat and gravy! Our riff on this underrated dish features a beef and veggie patty with a savory mushroom sauce.

½ lb (227 g) 90% lean ground beef

1 oz (30 g) salmon

1 medium (2 oz / 60 g) carrot, finely chopped

1 tbsp (9 g) roasted, unsalted sunflower seeds

½ tbsp (7½ ml) olive oil

1 cup (80 g) cremini mushrooms, thinly sliced

1 cup (240 ml) water

1 tbsp (9 g) oyster powder

1 tsp (3 g) carob powder

⅓ tsp (2 g) eggshell powder

¼ tsp (0.5 g) sea kelp powder

½ tbsp (3–4 g) oat flour

1. In a bowl, combine the beef, salmon, carrot, and sunflower seeds. Form into meatballs or patties the right size for your pup.

2. In a large saucepan over medium heat, drizzle the olive oil and add the mushrooms. Cook the mushrooms for about 5 minutes to soften.

3. Add the water and bring to a simmer.

4. Stir in the oyster powder, carob powder, eggshell powder, and sea kelp powder.

5. Carefully drop the beef patties into the simmering water. Cook for about 10 minutes total, flipping them over halfway, or until firm. Reduce heat to low.

6. Stir in oat flour to thicken the sauce.

7. Remove from the heat. Let the food cool slightly before portioning into servings for your dog. Cool completely before serving. Store any leftover portions in airtight containers in the fridge for up to 4 days.

Spaghetti Squash with Bison

GRAIN-FREE ❧ **HYPOALLERGENIC** ❧ **MAKES 1,800 CALORIES, 50% FROM FAT, 40% FROM PROTEIN, 10% FROM CARBOHYDRATE**

Spaghetti squash isn't just the name of a dish. It's the name of the actual type of gourd. Once cooked, spaghetti squash has a stringy, pasta-like texture that makes it a fun, low-carb substitute for the real thing. It's also very soft, making it an enjoyable meal for your aging best friend.

½ medium (about 2 lb / 908 g) spaghetti squash

3 tbsp (45 g) olive oil

1 lb (454 g) ground bison

1 (4¼ oz / 125 g) tin unsalted sardines in water, drained

1 oz (30 g) freeze-dried bison liver

2 tbsp (17 g) roasted, unsalted sunflower seeds

¾ tsp (5 g) ground eggshell

½ tsp (1 g) sea kelp powder

Handful of chopped fresh basil (optional)

1. Preheat the oven to 400°F (205°C). Line a rimmed baking sheet with parchment paper.

2. Using a large knife, very carefully cut the spaghetti squash in half lengthwise. Scoop out the seeds and ribbing. Place the squash cut sides down on the prepared baking sheet and bake for 40–50 minutes, or until tender. Remove from the heat and set aside to cool.

3. While the squash is baking, heat the olive oil in a pan over medium heat, then add the ground bison, sardines, liver, sunflower seeds, ground eggshell, and sea kelp powder. Cook until the bison is browned and cooked through. Remove from the heat.

4. Using a fork or spoon, scrape the spaghetti squash flesh from the skin into pasta-like strands.

5. Add the spaghetti squash strands to the pot with the meat filling, toss to combine, and garnish with basil. Let the food cool slightly before portioning into servings for your dog. Cool completely before serving. Store any leftover portions in airtight containers in the fridge for up to 4 days.

Turkey "Risotto" with Salmon

MAKES 1,525 CALORIES, 55% FROM FAT, 37% FROM PROTEIN, 8% FROM CARBOHYDRATE

For a low-carb risotto cooked to perfection, skip the rice and turn to the humble cauliflower. This dish features juicy turkey for flavor and veggies blended in for vitamins and fiber.

2 tbsp (30 g) olive oil

2 oz (60 g) salmon

1 lb (454 g) lean ground turkey

2 oz (60 g) chicken liver, chopped

3 cups (350 g) riced cauliflower

2 large eggs

¼ cup (30 g) wheat germ

1 cup (240 ml) water or dog-friendly broth

1 tbsp (9 g) oyster powder

½ tsp (1 g) sea kelp powder

¾ tsp (5 g) ground eggshell

1–2 basil leaves (optional)

1. Heat the olive oil in a large saucepan over medium heat. Add the salmon and cook for 3–4 minutes on each side, or until cooked through. Remove and set aside.

2. Add the turkey and chicken liver to the pan and cook for 5 minutes.

3. Add the riced cauliflower, eggs, wheat germ, and water or broth. Bring to a simmer and stir to break up the eggs. Cook for 5 minutes, or until the cauliflower is soft and the eggs are to your desired doneness.

4. Stir in the oyster powder, sea kelp powder, and ground eggshell. Remove from the heat and allow to cool. Top with the cooked salmon and basil leaves, if using.

5. When the food is cooled, portion into servings for your dog. Store any leftovers in airtight containers in the fridge for up to 4 days.

Salmon Casserole

MAKES 1,275 CALORIES, 47% FROM FAT, 41% FROM PROTEIN, 12% FROM CARBOHYDRATE

Turkey, salmon, and eggs make up this easy casserole dish that will have your dog doing parkour (as wildly as a senior dog can manage) in the kitchen like Edith as it bakes.

6 large eggs

½ lb (227 g) lean ground turkey

¼ lb (114 g) salmon

2 oz (60 g) chopped chicken liver

1 cup (100 g) broccoli florets

1 cup (120 g) chopped carrots

2 tbsp (12 g) wheat germ

1 tbsp (9 g) oyster powder

½ tsp (1 g) sea kelp powder

¾ tsp (5 g) ground eggshell

1. Preheat the oven to 350°F (175°C).

2. Combine all the ingredients with a few pulses in a food processor.

3. Transfer to a loaf pan or a deep 8-inch (20-cm) square baking dish and cover with a piece of parchment paper.

4. Bake for 45–55 minutes, or until internal temperature reaches 165°F (75°C).

5. Let the casserole cool slightly before portioning into servings for your dog. Cool completely before serving. Store any leftover portions in airtight containers in the fridge for up to 4 days.

Note: Instead of mixing it in, sprinkle the wheat germ on top of the casserole before baking for extra flair.

Chicken Fajitas

MAKES 1,250 CALORIES WITHOUT TORTILLAS OR GRAINS, 57% FROM FAT, 36% FROM PROTEIN, 7% FROM CARBOHYDRATE ❧ 1,450 CALORIES WITH ½ BATCH OF QUINOA TORTILLAS, 53% FROM FAT, 32% FROM PROTEIN, 15% FROM CARBOHYDRATE

Bell peppers and chicken are the base of our pup-friendly version of this famous Tex-Mex dish. Finely slicing and thoroughly cooking the vegetables and meat will make them easy to chew and digest, especially for older dogs with tooth decay. If your pup prefers beef, you can swap it for the chicken and this recipe will still meet AAFCO balance requirements. Bison can be used if your dog has allergies to common proteins.

1 lb (454 g) chicken breast strips or lean ground chicken

2 oz (60 g) chicken liver, chopped

2 oz (60 g) salmon

1 cup (150 g) thinly sliced (or diced) bell peppers

1 cup (80 g) button mushrooms, thinly sliced

2 tbsp (12 g) wheat germ

1 tbsp (9 g) oyster powder

½ tsp (1 g) sea kelp powder

¾ tsp (5 g) ground eggshell

Pinch of cumin, Ceylon cinnamon, and/or ground turmeric (optional)

½ cup water

2 tbsp (30 g) olive oil

½ batch Quinoa Tortillas (see Enchiladogs Verdes, page 203) or other grain for serving (optional)

1. Combine all the ingredients except the olive oil and optional Quinoa Tortillas or other grain in a pan and bring to a simmer over medium heat. Cook until the water is mostly absorbed, the meat is done, and the vegetables are soft, about 15 minutes.

2. Add the olive oil and toss to coat everything evenly. Let the mixture sizzle slightly before turning off the heat.

3. Let the mixture cool slightly before portioning into servings for your dog. Cool completely before serving. Optionally, serve with Quinoa Tortillas or other grain. Store any leftover portions in airtight containers in the fridge for up to 4 days.

Note: Blending the bell peppers and mushrooms up into a very fine paste, before adding them to the pan to cook, can be a beneficial way to feed picky eaters and dogs with more sensitive stomachs.

Venison and Blackberry Stuffing

GRAIN-FREE 🐾 MAKES 1,300 CALORIES, 43% FROM FAT, 44% FROM PROTEIN, 13% FROM CARBOHYDRATE

Inspired by a festive dish often seen on holiday dinner tables, this is a meal senior dogs can stuff their bellies with and still feel good afterward. Cubed sweet potato replaces the traditional bread, so no refined carbs are used. While venison is not widely available in grocery stores, these days it's easy to find online.

1 medium (2 oz / 60 g) carrot, cubed

½ small (4 oz / 120 g) sweet potato, cubed

3 tbsp (45 g) olive oil

1 tbsp (9 g) oyster powder

¾ tsp (5 g) ground eggshell

½ tsp (1 g) sea kelp powder

½ tsp (1 g) ground turmeric (optional)

½ tsp (1–2 g) cinnamon (optional)

1 lb (454 g) ground venison or venison stew chunks

1 (4¼ oz / 125 g) tin unsalted sardines in water, drained

¼ oz (7.5 g) freeze-dried beef liver, crushed

1 sprig rosemary (optional)

½ cup (120 ml) water or dog-friendly broth

2 oz (60 g) blackberries

1. Preheat the oven to 375°F (190°C).

2. In a Dutch oven or a large ovenproof pot with a lid, toss the carrot and sweet potato with the olive oil, oyster powder, ground eggshell, sea kelp powder, turmeric (if using), and Ceylon cinnamon (if using).

3. Add the venison (in clumps, if using ground meat), sardines, and liver and gently toss to distribute evenly. Add the rosemary sprig (if using) on top.

4. Pour in the water or broth, cover the pot, and bake for 1 hour.

5. Remove the rosemary sprig (if using) and top with the blackberries. Let the stuffing cool slightly before portioning into servings for your dog. Cool completely before serving. Store any leftover portions in airtight containers in the fridge for up to 4 days.

Athletes and Working Dogs

If your pup engages in very intense activities like agility trials or is a working dog active for many hours of the day, they'll need extra energy to sustain them. However, it's not simply a matter of more calories. The type of activity affects a dog's dietary requirements (and humans', too).[39]

When engaging in low-to-medium-intensity activity, both dogs and people prefer to burn fat for energy over carbs. However, there is a trade-off for this efficiency. Fats take longer to break down and utilize as energy. So, for very high-intensity activity, like running and sprinting, too much fat actually **decreases** top-end performance in speed and agility. Carbohydrates are the fastest source in those cases.

What does all this mean for your active pup? Working dogs benefit from higher-fat, higher-protein diets with minimal calories from carbohydrates, to sustain them for long hours of medium-intensity work. For athlete dogs, our formulations are lower in protein and fat and higher in carbohydrate than our worker formulations to provide top-end speed and agility. Here you'll find two recipes for athletes and two for working dogs to give them the energy their bodies need.

Shepup's Pie (for Athlete Dogs)

MAKES 2,150 CALORIES, 37% FROM FAT, 33% FROM PROTEIN, 30% FROM CARBOHYDRATE

While it takes its name from shepherd's pie, this recipe is formulated with athletes (not herders) in mind. If your dog needs to run and sprint, this Scottish favorite is for you. It's simple to make, utilizing frozen peas and carrots along with ground beef, and topped with a sweet potato crust that you can opt to broil for a golden-brown finishing touch.

1 lb (454 g) 90% lean ground beef

2 ounces (60 g) salmon

¼ ounce (7.5 g) freeze-dried beef liver

1½ cups (200 g) frozen peas and carrots

½ cup (50 g) oats

4 tbsp (35 g) roasted, unsalted sunflower seeds

1 tbsp (9 g) oyster powder

½ tsp (1 g) sea kelp powder

½ cup (120 ml) water

1 medium (14 oz / 400 g) sweet potato, cubed

1 large egg

¾ tsp (5 g) ground eggshell

1. Preheat the oven to 375°F (190°C).

2. Mix the ground beef, salmon, liver, peas and carrots, oats, sunflower seeds, oyster powder, sea kelp powder, and water in a 13 × 9-inch (33 × 23 cm) casserole dish or Dutch oven with a lid.

3. Cover and bake for 25–30 minutes, or until the sauce is bubbly and the meat is browned.

4. While the filling is baking, add the sweet potato cubes to a pot, cover completely with water, and bring to a boil. Simmer on medium-low heat for 10 minutes or until fork-tender. Drain and return the sweet potato cubes to the pot.

5. Add the egg and ground eggshell to the pot with the piping-hot sweet potato. Mash with a wooden spoon or potato masher until smooth.

6. Carefully remove the casserole dish from the oven. Stir the filling, breaking up any large chunks.

7. Spoon the mashed sweet potato on top of the filling, creating a thin layer that covers the entire dish. If you like, set the oven to broil. Return the casserole dish to the oven and broil for a few minutes, until the potato topping turns golden brown.

8. Let the Shepup's Pie cool slightly before portioning into servings for your dog. Cool completely before serving. Store any leftover portions in airtight containers in the fridge for up to 4 days.

Quick version: Add all the ingredients into a large pot with 3 cups (720 ml) of water and simmer on low, covered, for 20 minutes, or until the beef and sweet potatoes are cooked through.

Bison Sausage Stew (for Athlete Dogs)

MAKES 2,660 CALORIES, 41% FROM FAT, 32% FROM PROTEIN, 27% FROM CARBOHYDRATE

If your pup engages in very intense activities like agility trials and racing, this is the recipe for them. With higher carbohydrate content and lower fat than maintenance formulas, this recipe will give your dog the energy they need for top end speed and quickness.

1 lb (454 g) ground bison or stew meat

1½ cups (150 g) broccoli florets

¼ lb (114 g) salmon

½ cup (60 g) wheat germ

⅓ oz (9 g) freeze-dried beef liver

1½ tsp (7.5 g) ground eggshell

1 tbsp (9 g) oyster powder

½ tsp (1 g) sea kelp powder

3 tbsp (45 g) olive oil

3 cups (720 ml) water

1 cup (195 g) dry quinoa

1. Combine all the ingredients except the water and quinoa in a food processor and pulse until a paste forms.

2. Roll the mixture into small sausage shapes or meatballs.

3. Pour the water into a large pot and bring to a boil over medium-high heat. Once the pot is boiling, reduce the heat to low, add the sausages and quinoa, cover with a lid, and simmer for 15–20 minutes, or until the quinoa is cooked through.

4. Let the stew cool slightly before portioning into servings for your dog. Cool completely before serving. Store any leftover portions in airtight containers in the fridge for up to 4 days.

Pupeye's Spinach Patties (for Working Dogs)

GRAIN-FREE ☸ MAKES 1,650 CALORIES, 59% FROM FAT, 37% FROM PROTEIN, 4% FROM CARBOHYDRATE

Patrol, hunting, sledding, and herding are all activities where a dog is active for many hours of the day. This recipe is formulated for long hours of low-to-medium-intensity work where top-end speed and agility are not the main needs. These spinach and beef patties will help any highly active pup thrive.

1 lb (454 g) 90% lean ground beef

¼ lb (114 g) salmon

1 cup (100 g) spinach

2 large eggs

2 tbsp (30 g) olive oil

¼ oz (7.5 g) freeze-dried beef liver

2 tbsp (10 g) psyllium husk

⅓ cup (80 ml) water

2 tbsp (17 g) roasted, unsalted sunflower seeds

¾ tsp (5 g) ground eggshell

2 tbsp (17 g) oyster powder

½ tsp (1 g) sea kelp powder

Clarified butter or tallow, for greasing the pan

1. Combine all the ingredients except for the clarified butter/tallow in a food processor and pulse until finely minced. You want the mixture to stick together, but don't want it to turn into a paste. Alternatively, finely chop the ingredients with a knife and combine them in a bowl.

2. Scoop the mixture into balls (size appropriate for your dog to eat) and flatten into patties.

3. Heat a pan on medium-low heat. Drop in the clarified butter or tallow and swirl to coat the pan. Cook the patties for 4–5 minutes on each side, or until cooked through. Adding a splash of water to the pan can help them cook without burning.

4. Let the patties cool slightly before portioning into servings for your dog. Cool completely before serving and serve with adequate water. Store any leftover portions in airtight containers in the fridge for up to 4 days.

When feeding psyllium husk, make sure your dog is drinking enough water. We suggest adding a splash of water into their food before serving.

Tamadogyaki (for Working Dogs)

GRAIN-FREE 🐾 **MAKES 1,600 CALORIES, 58% FROM FAT, 39% FROM PROTEIN, 3% FROM CARBOHYDRATE**

Eggs are a near perfect food for a working pup—and they're a versatile component of many dishes the world over. Tamagoyaki is a beautiful Japanese omelet, traditionally cooked in a rectangular pan and rolled. You don't need a fancy pan or technique to make this dish, but rolling it makes it easy to slice, portion, and serve. It's dense and delicious and will help your dog hike, work, and move for hours on end.

1 lb (454 g) ground chicken

1 (4¼ oz / 125 g) tin unsalted sardines in water, drained

1 cup (120 g) finely chopped broccoli

1 cup (100 g) chopped spinach

2 tbsp (10 g) psyllium husk

½ cup (120 ml) water

¾ tsp (5 g) ground eggshell

½ tsp (1 g) sea kelp powder

2 tbsp (30 g) olive oil

6 large eggs

1. In a bowl, combine the ground chicken, sardines, broccoli, spinach, psyllium husk, water, ground eggshell, and sea kelp powder.

2. Heat the olive oil in a large pan over medium heat. Add the chicken mixture and cook until the chicken is done, about 10 minutes. Transfer the mixture to another bowl.

3. Whisk the eggs in a separate bowl, then pour a small amount into the pan (enough to coat the entire pan). If using a tamagoyaki pan, you may need to cook a few batches. Spread the chicken mixture evenly onto one side of the eggs. As the eggs begin to set, using a spatula, roll the omelet from one end to the other. Pour more of the egg mix into the now empty space in the pan. As they start to set, continue rolling until the chicken filling is completely wrapped in egg.

4. Let the omelet cook on all sides to set through.

5. Let the omelet cool slightly before portioning into servings for your dog. Cool completely before serving and serve with adequate water. Store any leftover portions in airtight containers in the fridge for up to 4 days.

When feeding psyllium husk, make sure your dog is drinking enough water. We suggest adding a splash of water into their food before serving.

Weight Loss

Many dogs are overweight. Processed foods, overfeeding, and a sedentary lifestyle can contribute to this. You can support a healthy weight by offering your dog real-food recipes specifically formulated for weight loss.

Diet is the most effective intervention for weight management. Here are our top tips for healthy weight loss in dogs:

1. Start with high-quality food. Both the amount and type of food matter! Convincing research suggests that low-carbohydrate, high-protein, high-fiber diets are most effective to help pups shed a few pounds.[40]

2. Be patient. Start by giving your dog the *recommended calories* per day (see the feeding guide on page 20) for their ideal weight. Keep track of their weight and waistline every week. If they are not losing about 1 percent of body weight per week, adjust their portion size down slowly. (For a medium-sized dog, for instance, you can reduce portions by one to two spoonfuls or about 5–10 percent.) Then wait one to two weeks to see if their weight improves and reassess.

3. Cut out treats and scraps. If you live with family or housemates, it's helpful to make only one person responsible for feeding to ensure you're staying on track.

4. Stay strong. Dogs will always act like they are starving, especially when you reduce their food intake. Just remember that you're saving your dog from painful disease and suffering.

While diet is paramount, also remember that movement matters, too. Make sure your pup gets plenty of exercise every day.

These formulas boast more protein than our Adult Maintenance recipes, limit carbohydrates to less than 10 percent, and are still fully balanced to meet AAFCO standards. For fiber, which helps with digestion and satiation, we add psyllium husk fiber to many of these recipes. Psyllium husk fiber is great for weight loss and can also help with upset stomachs. It's important that psyllium husk is consumed with a sufficient amount of water, so make sure your pup always has some available. If they don't like drinking water, add a little to each of their meals. We suggest feeding these recipes for a few months to hit your pup's weight goals. Once your dog is back to a healthy weight, you can offer them other recipes again.

Duck "Noodle" Soup

GRAIN-FREE 🐾 **MAKES 670 CALORIES, 52% FROM FAT, 43% FROM PROTEIN, 5% FROM CARBOHYDRATE**

Skinless duck breast is a lean cut of meat that is perfect for weight loss. In this soup, it's paired with baby bok choy to provide nutrients and fiber, and egg "noodles" for extra protein without the carbs. To simplify the recipe, you can skip the step of making our Egg Noodles (page 50) and simply poach two eggs directly in the broth in step 4 with the bok choy.

Clarified butter, tallow, or other cooking oil

½ lb (227 g) duck breast, skin removed

2 cups (480 ml) water or dog-friendly broth

1 tbsp (8 g) oyster powder

¼ tsp (1.5 g) ground eggshell

½ tsp (1 g) sea kelp powder

1 tbsp (5 g) psyllium husk

½ cup (40 g) cremini or enoki mushrooms (optional)

1 head (3.5 oz / 100 g) baby bok choy

½ tin (2 oz / 60 g) unsalted sardines in water, drained

1 batch Egg Noodles (page 50)

1 tbsp (15 g) olive oil

1. Heat the frying oil in a pan over medium-high heat until hot but not smoky. Sear the duck for 4–5 minutes on each side, or until medium rare or the internal temperature is 140°F (60°C). Transfer the duck to a plate and set aside.

2. Pour the water or broth into the same pan and bring to a boil. Dissolve the oyster powder, ground eggshell, sea kelp powder, and psyllium husk in the water.

3. Add the mushrooms (if using). Cook for 10 minutes.

4. Add the bok choy. Cook for 2–3 minutes.

5. Cut the duck into thin slices.

6. Remove the broth from the heat. Add the sardines, Egg Noodles, and sliced duck.

7. Let the soup cool slightly and drizzle the olive oil over the top before portioning into servings for your dog. Cool completely before serving. Store any leftover portions in airtight containers in the fridge for up to 4 days.

Chicken and Cauliflower Fried Rice

GRAIN-FREE 🐾 **MAKES 1,575 CALORIES, 56% FROM FAT, 34% FROM PROTEIN, 10% FROM CARBOHYDRATE**

Delight your pup with this fried rice–inspired dish that's studded with green peas, bok choy, and savory chicken. Cauliflower is low in carbs and high in fiber, while chicken breast is low in fat and high in protein. This dish will satisfy even the hungriest canine dieters.

1 tsp (5 g) tallow or coconut oil

1 lb (454 g) ground chicken

2 oz (60 g) chicken liver, chopped into bite-sized pieces

2 cups (220 g) riced cauliflower

2 heads (7 oz / 200 g) baby bok choy, chopped

1 cup (150 g) frozen peas

2 tbsp (30 g) olive oil

4 large eggs

2 tbsp (10 g) psyllium husk

1 tbsp (9 g) oyster powder

¾ tsp (5 g) ground eggshell

½ tsp (1 g) sea kelp powder

1. In a large wok or frying pan, heat the tallow or coconut oil over medium-high heat. Add the ground chicken and liver and cook, stirring and breaking them up into crumbles as they brown, until mostly done, about 5 minutes.

2. Add the cauliflower, bok choy, peas, and a splash of water to help the veggies steam. Cook, stirring occasionally, for 5 minutes, or until the veggies are soft.

3. Scoot the meat and veggies to the side of the pan. Drizzle the olive oil into the pan, then add the eggs. Scramble the eggs in the pan and cook until the eggs begin to set, 1–2 minutes. Toss the eggs with the chicken and veggies to combine everything and cook until the eggs are done, about 1 more minute. Remove from heat.

4. Add the psyllium husk, oyster powder, ground eggshell, and sea kelp powder. Toss to evenly distribute.

5. Let the fried rice cool slightly before portioning into servings for your dog. Cool completely before serving and serve with adequate water. Store any leftover portions in airtight containers in the fridge for up to 4 days.

When feeding psyllium husk, make sure your dog is drinking enough water. We suggest adding a splash of water into their food before serving.

Seafood and Spinach Furttata

GRAIN-FREE 🐾 **MAKES 975 CALORIES, 53% FROM FAT, 43% FROM PROTEIN, 4% FROM CARBOHYDRATE**

Packed with protein and healthy omega-3 fatty acids, this dog-friendly frittata with salmon, shrimp, and green veggies is so delicious your pup will never know they're on a diet.

6 large eggs

1 tbsp (5 g) psyllium husk

¼ cup (60 ml) water

1 tbsp (9 g) oyster powder

½ tsp (3 g) ground eggshell

½ tsp (1 g) sea kelp powder

1 tbsp (15 g) olive oil

¼ lb (114 g) shrimp

2 oz (60 g) salmon, chopped into bite-sized pieces

½ cup (50 g) chopped spinach

1. In a bowl, whisk the eggs with the psyllium husk, water, oyster powder, ground eggshell, and sea kelp powder.

2. Heat the olive oil in a large pan over low heat. Sauté the shrimp and salmon for 1–2 minutes, then add the spinach. Splash in some water, cover with a lid, and allow the seafood and veggies to steam for 3–4 minutes.

3. Pour the egg mixture on top, covering everything in the pan. Cook until the bottom is set, 5–8 minutes, then flip the frittata over. You can fold it or cut it in half before flipping to make it easier to turn over.

4. Cook for 1–2 more minutes, or until the other side is just set.

5. Let the frittata cool slightly before portioning into servings for your dog. Cool completely before serving and serve with adequate water. Store any leftover portions in airtight containers in the fridge for up to 4 days.

When feeding psyllium husk, make sure your dog is drinking enough water. We suggest adding a splash of water into their food before serving.

Chicken Asparagus Bake

GRAIN-FREE ☙ **MAKES 1,300 CALORIES, 52% FROM FAT, 44% FROM PROTEIN, 4% FROM CARBOHYDRATE**

Who doesn't love a sheet pan supper? Asparagus, spinach, and chicken come together for a fully balanced, low-carb meal that's simple to throw together and bake on one pan.

1 lb (454 g) boneless, skinless chicken breasts

3½ oz (100 g) chicken liver, chopped

2 cups (360 g) chopped asparagus

2 cups (150 g) button mushrooms, diced

½ cup (50 g) chopped spinach

1 tbsp (9 g) roasted, unsalted sunflower seeds

¼ cup (60 ml) water

5 large eggs

1 tbsp (9 g) oyster powder

½ tsp (1 g) sea kelp powder

¾ tsp (5 g) ground eggshell

1. Preheat the oven to 350°F (175°C). Line a rimmed baking sheet with parchment paper.

2. Spread out the chicken, chicken liver, asparagus, mushrooms, spinach, and sunflower seeds on the prepared baking sheet. Pour the water over everything.

3. Bake for 25–30 minutes, or until the chicken is cooked through and the vegetables are tender.

4. Make five spaces among the chicken and veggies and crack the eggs in. Bake for another 5–6 minutes, or until the eggs are just set.

5. Sprinkle the oyster powder, sea kelp powder, and ground eggshell on top. Shred the chicken with two forks and toss to combine everything together.

6. Let the food cool slightly before portioning into servings for your dog. Cool completely before serving. Store any leftover portions in airtight containers in the fridge for up to 4 days.

Asparagus may be more difficult for some dogs to digest in large chunks. Finely chopping it or pulsing in a food processor before cooking is great if your dog is sensitive.

Bison Barkbacoa

GRAIN-FREE 🐾 **MAKES 1,675 CALORIES, 55% FROM FAT, 40% FROM PROTEIN, 5% FROM CARBOHYDRATE**

Barbacoa is one of our favorites for tacos or burritos. Slow cooking makes the meat both tender and juicy. For extra flair, serve the succulent barbacoa on top of egg "tortillas" with fresh garnishes, and pair with a Pineapple Pawgarita (page 285). Short on time? Use ground bison instead of stew meat. It will cook in 10 minutes.

Barbacoa

1 lb (454 g) bison stew meat, cubed

1 cup (150 g) chopped green bell peppers

2 tbsp (17 g) roasted, unsalted sunflower seeds

1 tsp (3 g) carob powder

3½ oz (100 g) salmon

½ cup (50 g) chopped spinach

2 tbsp (17 g) oyster powder

¾ tsp (5 g) ground eggshell

½ tsp (1 g) sea kelp powder

Egg "Tortillas"

3 large eggs

2 tbsp (30 g) olive oil

Garnishes

2–3 sprigs of cilantro (optional)

Chopped radishes (optional)

Cucumber slices (optional)

Barbacoa

1. Combine the bison, bell peppers, sunflower seeds, and carob powder in a pot. Cover with water and bring to a boil on medium heat. Reduce the heat to low and simmer for at least 45 minutes or longer for more tender meat.

2. When the barbacoa is tender, add the salmon, spinach, oyster powder, ground eggshell, and sea kelp powder and stir to combine. Cook for 5–10 more minutes, or until the salmon is cooked through.

3. If you skip the egg tortillas, whisk the eggs and add directly to the pot along with the olive oil. Cook for 2 minutes. Shred the bison meat and salmon with two forks.

4. Let the food cool slightly before portioning into servings for your dog. Cool completely before serving.

5. Optional: Serve the barbacoa on top of egg tortillas (see steps below) and garnish with cilantro, radishes, and cucumbers. Store any leftover portions in airtight containers in the fridge for up to 4 days.

Egg "Tortillas"

1. In a large mixing bowl, thoroughly whisk the eggs.

2. Heat a nonstick frying pan on medium heat and drizzle in the olive oil a little at a time, depending on how many batches you need to make.

3. Arrange a few heat-safe circle egg molds in the pan. Pour a small amount of egg into each mold to form a thin layer.

4. Cook until mostly set, about 2–3 minutes, then remove the molds, flip, and cook for a few seconds on the other side. Transfer the egg tortillas to a plate and repeat until all the eggs have been cooked.

Meals for Foodie Pups

For many people, especially those who are not aware of how wonderful dogs' sense of smell is, the idea of foodie pups might sound absurd. Because dogs were bred to love and adore us, most accept eating the same food day in and day out. (That monotony might make them bored or angry if they thought more like people!) Since they are so good-natured, we can easily forget how much food means to them.

This section is all about paying homage to dogs' experience of food. We curated and adapted many of these recipes directly from our social media channel, Thecedlife. These recipes aren't about daily feeding, nutrition, or practicality—they are really just about being silly and having fun. (They aren't balanced to AAFCO standards, so make sure your dog gets a varied diet that includes the key nutrients they need; offering our Balanced Meals and Supermeals recipes on other days will take care of this.) Despite the silliness, there are still benefits to be had. Aside from giving your pups enjoyment and nutrition, cooking for them is a low-stakes way to practice your culinary skills *and* may encourage you to broaden your own palate. If you mess up, no worries—your pups will still love the results!

Dining Experiences

We curated some of the most popular casual and fancy dining experiences from our channel for this section. This is a collection of our favorite meals made in the most dog-friendly ways. Most recipes are pretty simple and can be a weekend activity or a way for you to bond with your best furry friend.

For example, on a cold day we love starting a pot of pho broth in the morning, simmering it on the stove all day, and then slurping up the flavorful noodles for dinner. Making pizza on a Friday night can now be a dog-inclusive activity, too. It's time we shared these experiences with our pups, because they're a part of the family and real food is good for them!

Pup Bread

MAKES 2 SMALL LOAVES, 85 CALORIES WITH OAT FLOUR OR TAPIOCA STARCH

Fresh bread may be one of the world's most delicious human foods, but your pup doesn't need all those carbs. Instead of wheat flour, egg whites are the foundation of this pup bread. Optionally, you can add oat flour or tapioca starch to give the bread a bit more structure. Pup bread is used as buns for the Diner Burger and Fries (page 182), and the baguette in your Bark Mi (page 187). The egg whites can be a little tricky to work with, but patience and time make all the difference—and remember that your pup will love it even if it's not perfect.

3 egg whites (about 90 g)

2 tbsp (14 g) oat flour or tapioca starch (optional, but recommended)

1. Preheat your oven to 350°F (175°C). Line a baking sheet or mold with parchment paper.

2. Make sure your bowl and whisk are clean and dry. Whisk the egg whites in the bowl for 3–4 minutes or longer, or until they form shiny, stiff peaks. They will get foamy first, then slowly start to thicken. When you remove the whisk, the "peak" formed by the egg whites should remain standing.

3. Sprinkle in the oat flour or tapioca starch (if using), and gently fold it in with a spatula until just combined.

4. Using a spoon or spatula, scoop the egg whites into the prepared molds or onto the prepared baking sheet and form them into your desired bread shapes. This takes a steady hand and patience as the egg whites are delicate and not easy to work with. Work quickly and don't spend too long shaping or they will start to melt and deflate.

5. Bake for about 20 minutes, or until golden brown. Slice the bread and use right away. The bread is best served fresh, within 1 day of baking.

Ketchpup

GRAIN-FREE ❧ **HYPOALLERGENIC** ❧ **MAKES 3 CUPS, 500 CALORIES**

A dog-friendly version of the classic condiment, Ketchpup is a stand-in for ketchup, tomato sauce, chili sauce, and more! Though it's a beautiful red sauce, it's not just for decoration. Sweet potatoes and beets are rich in vitamins and minerals as well as soluble fiber that helps digestion. This sauce also adds moisture to your dog's food, just like sauces do in people's foods. You'll see Ketchpup in many of our recipes, so go ahead and make a batch and freeze it for later.

1 small (7 oz / 200 g) beet

1 medium (18 oz / 500 g) sweet potato, chopped

¼–½ cup (60–120 ml) water or dog-friendly broth

1. Fill a steamer pot with water and bring to a boil over medium-high heat.

2. Steam the beet and sweet potato until fork-tender. You can steam them whole (30–40 minutes) or halve or quarter them first to speed up the cooking time. Keep in mind that beets take slightly longer than sweet potatoes to soften. Avoid boiling as this will cause the beet to lose its color.

3. Remove the skins (they glide off easily after cooking).

4. Transfer the sweet potato and beet to a blender. Add the water or broth a little bit at a time and puree until smooth. Add more water as needed to make the sauce your desired consistency.

5. Let the Ketchpup cool before using it in a recipe. Store any leftover sauce in airtight containers in the fridge for up to 4 days. Since this makes a large batch, freeze some portions for up to six months in ice cube trays or freezer bags for convenient thawing.

Pumpkin or butternut squash can be used in place of sweet potato.

Diner Burger and Fries

MAKES 1 BURGER PLUS FRIES, 350 CALORIES

There's nothing more American than a burger and fries. Create the ultimate pup sliders by forming our Pup Bread recipe (page 178) into burger buns. Sweet potato fries are made complete with Ketchpup (page 181), a dog-friendly version of our favorite companion to fries. This recipe is portioned to make one perfect Diner Burger, and a 2 oz (60 g) patty is a good amount for a medium-sized dog. For small dogs, this could be two portions.

Sweet Potato Fries

½ small (4 oz / 120 g) sweet potato

1 small sprig (2–3 leaflets) rosemary, finely chopped (optional)

1 tsp (4 g) grated Parmesan cheese (optional)

Diner Burger

2 oz (60 g) lean ground beef

1 slice of your dog's favorite cheese (we use Swiss Emmental cheese)

1 egg or quail egg (optional)

Assembly

½ batch Pup Bread (page 178), shaped into a bun

A few thin slices of cucumber

Drizzle of Ketchpup (page 181)

1. Make the fries: Preheat the oven to 325°F (165°C). Line a baking sheet with parchment paper.

2. Peel the sweet potato and slice into fry-shaped pieces that your dog can easily eat.

3. Transfer the sweet potato pieces to the prepared baking sheet. Bake for 25–30 minutes, or until the sweet potato is thoroughly softened.

4. Make the burger: While the fries are baking, form a patty with the ground beef.

5. In a pan, cook the patty on medium heat for about 3 minutes. (If using very lean beef or bison, you may need to grease the pan with some frying oil.) Flip and place a slice of cheese on top. Cook for another 3 minutes, or until the cheese has melted and the burger is cooked through. Remove from the heat.

6. If you're topping your burger with an egg, fry the egg in the same pan until it's done to your pup's liking (for a large egg, it takes 2–3 minutes for the white to set while the yolk remains runny).

7. Assemble: Place the burger on the Pup Bread bun and top with the optional egg, cucumber slices, and Ketchpup (or top however you want). If you like, toss the fries with the optional rosemary and Parmesan cheese for extra flair and flavor.

8. Allow the burger and fries to cool to a safe temperature and serve.

Spawghetti and Meatballs

MAKES 750 CALORIES

The classic combo of spaghetti and meatballs is in (almost) everyone's dinner rotation for a reason. It's a crowd-pleaser and easy to make. Set a place at the table for your pup, with their own plate of specially made Spawghetti, to enjoy alongside you. If you're in a rush, use ½ can of plain pumpkin puree for the sauce instead of Ketchpup.

½ lb (227 g) lean ground beef

1 medium (2 oz / 60 g) carrot, grated

¼ cup (25 g) finely chopped spinach

½ cup (45 g) rolled oats

⅛ tsp oregano (optional)

⅛ tsp thyme (optional)

2 cups (480 ml) water

½ cup (120 g) Ketchpup (page 181)

1 tbsp (15 g) olive oil (optional)

1 batch Egg Noodles (page 50)

1 tbsp grated Parmesan, for sprinkling (optional)

1. Combine the ground beef, carrot, spinach, rolled oats, oregano (if using), and thyme (if using) in a bowl.

2. Form ½- inch to 1-inch (2–3 cm) meatballs and set aside on a plate.

3. Bring the water to a boil in a large saucepan over medium heat.

4. Add the meatballs. Reduce the heat to low and simmer the meatballs for 6–8 minutes, flipping them halfway if needed.

5. When the water has mostly evaporated, add the Ketchpup and toss to coat the meatballs in the sauce.

6. Turn off the heat and stir in the optional olive oil.

7. Serve the meatballs and sauce on top of the Egg Noodles. Sprinkle Parmesan on top, if using. Cool completely before serving. Store any leftover portions in airtight containers in the fridge for up to 4 days.

Bark Mi

MAKES 2 SMALL BARK MI, 350 CALORIES

Vietnamese sandwiches mix the best of Asian and European flavors: crispy bread with pâté, cold cuts, and pickles creates a unique combination. For pups, we use our dog-friendly Pup Bread and a simple chicken liver pâté. This dish involves a bit of work but is both beautiful and delicious.

1 oz (30 g) chicken liver

1 tbsp (15 ml) water, more if needed

Clarified butter or tallow, for frying

1 small (about 3½ oz / 100 g) steak

1 batch Pup Bread (page 178), shaped into 2 small baguettes

Handful (1 oz / 30 g) of thinly sliced carrots

Handful (1 oz / 30 g) of thinly sliced cucumbers

Handful (1 oz / 30 g) of thinly sliced red bell pepper or mini sweet peppers

1. Make the pâté: Place the chicken liver in a small pot and cover with water. Bring the water to a boil, then simmer on low for 10–15 minutes, until the chicken liver is cooked through.

2. In a blender or food processor, combine the cooked chicken liver and 1 tbsp (15 ml) water. Blend into a smooth paste, adding a little more water if needed.

3. Sear the steak: Heat up a pan on medium. Drop in the clarified butter or tallow. Sear the steak for 2 minutes on each side. Set aside to rest for 5 minutes.

4. Assemble: Thinly slice the steak. Slice each Pup Bread baguette in half lengthwise. Spread on a generous layer of chicken liver pâté. Then top with the sliced steak, carrots, cucumbers, and peppers and close the sandwiches.

5. Let the sandwiches cool completely before serving. For fast eaters and smaller dogs, chop up the sandwich into bite-sized pieces first.

Bibimpup

MAKES 2,000 CALORIES

Inspired by the Korean mixed rice dish bibimbap, Bibimpup is a vibrant rice bowl with bright, crunchy veggies, beef, and an egg on top. Optionally, top it with a spoonful of Dogchujang (aka Ketchpup, page 181).

¼ cup (50 g) uncooked rice, washed

1 small (1 oz /30 g) carrot, julienned

¼ cup (25 g) chopped spinach

Coconut oil

¼ lb (113 g) lean ground beef

2 oz (60 g) beef heart, chopped into bite-sized pieces (optional)

1 large egg

¼ cup (25 g) cucumber, julienned

Pinch of sesame seeds

1 tbsp (15 g) Dogchujang sauce (optional; use Ketchpup, page 181)

1. Cook the rice according to package directions.

2. Meanwhile, fill a saucepan halfway with water and bring to a boil over medium heat.

3. Add the carrot to blanch for about 1 minute. Remove with a slotted spoon and set aside.

4. Add the spinach to the boiling water to blanch for about 1 minute. Remove and set aside. Pour out the water and return the pot to the heat.

5. Melt a small amount of coconut oil in the pot, and add the beef and beef heart (if using). Cook for about 8 minutes, or until browned. Remove and set aside.

6. Crack the egg into the pan and cook it until just set, about 5 minutes. Cover the pan to help it steam without needing to be flipped over.

7. Assemble the bowl by topping the rice with the beef, beef heart, carrot, spinach, cucumber, fried egg, and sesame seeds. Optionally, add a dollop of Dogchujang sauce.

8. Stir the ingredients in the bowl and let the Bibimpup cool completely before portioning and serving. Store any leftover portions in airtight containers in the fridge for up to 4 days.

Pup Pho

MAKES 2 BOWLS, 500 CALORIES WITH MEAT FROM SOUP BONES

When it's cold outside or we are under the weather, pho is one of those dishes that help warm the soul. With a long-simmered broth, this soup is a labor of love. But pho loves you back because it's highly customizable, which means you can pick and choose your (pup's) favorite ingredients and toppings.

For soup bones, we like using beef ribs because they have meat on them that can be served in the soup. Adding chicken or turkey bones creates an even richer flavor. Instead of making meatballs, you can ladle the hot broth onto thin slices of raw steak, as done in pho restaurants. Serve with lots of Srirachow (aka Ketchpup, page 181).

Pho Broth

1 bone-in beef short rib and/or 1 turkey wing

1 slice fresh ginger (optional)

1 small Ceylon cinnamon stick (optional)

Pho Toppings

1 oz (30 g) dry rice noodles

2 oz (60 g) lean ground beef, formed into small meatballs

¼ oz (7 g) freeze-dried beef liver

Small handful (1 oz / 20 g) of broccoli sprouts or mung bean sprouts

1–2 basil leaves

Drizzle of Srirachow (aka Ketchpup, page 181)

1. Place the meaty bone(s) in a pot and cover it completely with water. Bring the pot to a boil on high heat.

2. Once a boil has been reached, carefully remove the bone(s) and rinse them under cold water to remove any scum. Pour out the cooking water and rinse the pot clean as well.

3. Return the bone(s) to the pot and cover with water again. If you're using spices, add the ginger and cinnamon stick now. Bring the pot to a boil on high heat, then turn the heat down to low and cover. Simmer for 8 hours, keeping an eye on the water level and adding more if it gets low.

4. Remove and discard the ginger, cinnamon stick, and all bones. Leave the meat from the bone(s) in the pot.

5. Before serving, in a separate pot, prepare the rice noodles according to the package directions and transfer them to two small dog bowls.

6. Add meatballs to the pho broth and cook for about 3 minutes, or until cooked through, and transfer them to the dog bowls.

7. On top of the rice noodles and meatballs, add the beef liver, sprouts, and basil, as well as any meat from the soup bone(s).

8. Carefully ladle the still-boiling broth into the bowls, covering the noodles and toppings. The sprouts get gently cooked by the hot broth for better digestion. Top with Srirachow.

9. Cool completely before serving. Refrigerate the remaining broth and use within 4 days. If making a large batch, pour the remaining broth into silicone molds and store in the freezer for up to 6 months. Extra broth comes in handy!

Quick version: Skip the long wait and use powdered bone broth to make a quick soup. Simmer with cinnamon and ginger (if using) for 15 minutes.

SRIRACHOW
CHOW
CHOW
SRIRACHOW
SRIRACHOW

Don't feed your dog the bones from the broth!

Pawgazy Pie

MAKES 1 PIE, 1,300 CALORIES

Looking for a very special pie to bake during the cold winter season? This is the one! Stargazy pie is a traditional Cornish dish that gets its name from its unique appearance: small fish are baked under the pastry with their heads poking through the crust, so they seem to be looking at the stars. While this may not be a very appealing pie for many people, the fish heads are a doggy favorite.

Crust

1 cup (100 g) oat flour

1 tbsp (15 g) olive oil, beef tallow, clarified butter, or coconut oil (optional; see note)

5 tbsp (75 ml) water, more if needed

6 dried fish (sprats, minnows, or sardines)

Filling

2 large eggs, soft-boiled

1 (4¼ oz / 125 g) tin unsalted sardines in water, drained

¼ cup (40 g) riced cauliflower

¼ cup (40 g) frozen peas

¼ cup (60 g) plain yogurt

Glaze

1 large egg (optional)

1. Preheat the oven to 350°F (175°C).

2. Combine the oat flour and the oil, tallow, or clarified butter in a bowl. Use your fingers to make sure the fat and flour are well incorporated. Add the water 1 tbsp (15 ml) at a time, mixing with your hands until a dough forms.

3. Roll out the dough into a slab and cut out a circle to fit the top of your pie pan. Set aside.

4. In another bowl, combine the 2 soft-boiled eggs, sardines, cauliflower, peas, and yogurt. Mix until you have what looks like egg salad.

5. Fill a 6-inch (15 cm) pie pan (2 inches / 6 cm deep) with the filling.

6. Carefully cover the filling with the crust. Cut six small slits in the crust that you can stick the fish heads or tails in, but don't stick them in yet!

7. If you like, whisk 1 egg in a small bowl and brush the top of the crust with it. This is optional but will help the crust brown nicely.

8. Bake for 30–45 minutes, or until the filling is bubbling and the crust is golden brown.

9. Remove from the oven and carefully insert the dried fish into the slits in the crust.

10. Let the pie cool slightly before portioning into servings for your dog. Cool completely before serving. Store any leftover portions in airtight containers in the fridge for up to 4 days.

Note: We like adding the fat to the crust in this recipe, but it's optional. You can omit it altogether and your crust will still come together with just water, though it may come out crunchier.

Pawlifornia Roll

MAKES 4 ROLLS, 700 CALORIES

Sushi night is fun and interactive, and an event that can be enjoyed by people and dogs together. All you need to do is cook up some rice and slice some of your favorite sashimi-grade fish. Prepare your ingredients nigiri-style—simply laying your fish on top of a mound of rice—or wrap them all together in toasted nori for a nutritious meal. If you opt to make our Pawlifornia Roll, you will need plastic wrap; although not required, a sushi mat will make things easy.

1 cup (100 g) cooked rice

1 tsp (5 g) olive oil

2 sheets unsalted roasted nori

Your Choice of Sushi Fillings

Pinch of sesame seeds (optional)

2 ounces (60 g) steak

2 ounces (60 g) sashimi-grade salmon* or tuna

1 (4¼ oz / 125 g) tin unsalted sardines in water, drained

Handful (2 oz / 60 g) of sliced cucumbers

1 oz (30 g) salmon egg roe (optional)

½ ounce (15 g) cooked, mashed peas (optional, for Pawsabi)

1. Mix the cooked rice with the olive oil in a bowl and cool.

2. Lay out a piece of plastic wrap on a sushi mat or clean tea towel.

3. Place half a sheet of nori on the plastic wrap.

4. Spread a thin layer of rice over the nori. Sprinkle with sesame seeds (if using), and flip the entire thing over so that the rice side faces down on the plastic wrap.

5. Add one-quarter of your fillings in a thin line across the nori, against the bottom edge.

6. Begin rolling, pulling the mat taut as you go. When you come to the end of the roll, remove the mat and roll it a few times in the cling wrap to help everything stick together.

7. Remove the cling wrap and slice the roll into rounds. If you like, top each round with a salmon egg.

8. Repeat steps 3–7 with the remaining nori, rice, and sushi fillings.

9. Serve your sushi with some Pawsabi (mushy peas) on the side. Sushi is best consumed immediately.

Rolling Sushi

*Never feed raw or undercooked wild salmon to your dogs unless it is sashimi grade (treated for parasites and frozen at −4°F/−20°C or below for at least seven days) and you know its source. Wild-caught salmon (and other fish) caught in the Pacific Northwest of the United States are often infected with Neorickettsia helminthoeca, an organism that can give your dog salmon poisoning disease. The good news is that thoroughly cooking the salmon eliminates this risk entirely. If you're unsure about the source of your salmon, cook it to be safe. It will still be tasty and full of wonderful omega-3 fatty acids!

Pawlifornia Roll | 194

Pawsta Trio—Green Pupsto, Dogka Sauce, and Carbarknara

Although we sometimes use store-bought pasta for the dogs, making fresh Pawsta at home is our preferred option as we can use fresh eggs and our favorite oat flour.

Of course, no Pawsta is complete without a sputacular sauce. Great pasta doesn't have to be complicated and our Green Pupsto, Dogka Sauce, and Carbarknara can each be made in just a few minutes.

Pawsta

MAKES 450 CALORIES

1 large egg

1 cup (100 g) oat flour, plus more as needed and for rolling

1. Crack the egg into a medium bowl and whisk well.

2. Add the oat flour ¼ cup (about 25 g) at a time, mixing with your hands until a dough forms. The dough should be soft but not too sticky, and you should be able to shape it and roll it out. Add more flour if needed. If it becomes dry, knead in a splash of water.

3. Dump your dough onto a flat surface dusted with more oat flour. Roll the dough out into a very thin slab.

4. Cut out your desired shapes. Set the noodles aside, dusting them with more flour to prevent sticking. (At this point, freeze any extras you aren't using right away.)

5. You can cook the Pawsta directly in soups and stews. If your dish requires cooked pasta, bring a pot of water to a boil over medium-high heat. Add the pasta to the boiling water and cook for 3–5 minutes. It should cook fast, but if your Pawsta is on the thicker side, give it an extra minute or so.

6. Remove from the heat and set aside a few tablespoons of the Pawsta cooking water to use in the sauce(s). Drain the Pawsta and use it in your dish. Store any leftover portions in airtight containers in the fridge for up to 4 days.

Green Pupsto

MAKES 250 CALORIES

5 basil leaves
½ cup (50 g) spinach
1 tbsp (9 g) roasted, unsalted sunflower seeds
1 tbsp (15 g) olive oil
1 tbsp (10 g) grated Parmesan cheese

1. Blend all the ingredients together except the Parmesan cheese. Add in a splash of water if needed to thin the sauce out.

2. Heat a saucepan on medium-low. Add the Pupsto with a few tablespoons of hot Pawsta cooking water and your cooked Pawsta. Reduce the heat to low and toss to evenly coat the Pawsta with the sauce.

3. Top with the Parmesan cheese. Cool completely before serving.

Dogka Sauce

MAKES 125 CALORIES

½ cup (100 g) plain pumpkin puree
2 tbsp (30 g) plain full-fat yogurt
1 tbsp (10 g) grated Parmesan cheese
1 basil leaf, for garnish

1. Heat a saucepan on medium-low. Combine the pumpkin puree and yogurt in the pan with a few tablespoons of hot Pawsta cooking water and your cooked Pawsta. Reduce the heat to low and toss to evenly coat the Pawsta with the sauce.

2. Top with the Parmesan cheese and garnish with a basil leaf. Cool completely before serving.

Carbarknara

MAKES 300 CALORIES

2 oz (60 g) ground beef
2 egg yolks
1 tbsp (10 g) grated Parmesan cheese

1. Heat a saucepan on medium-low and brown the ground beef, breaking it up into crumbles with a wooden spoon as it cooks, about 5 minutes.

2. Turn the heat off and stir in the egg yolks with a few tablespoons of hot Pawsta cooking water and your cooked Pawsta. Toss to evenly coat the Pawsta with the sauce.

3. Top with the Parmesan cheese. Cool completely before serving.

Pupza Party

GRAIN-FREE 🐾 MAKES 3 PIZZAS, 500 CALORIES

The crust on our Pupza is based on our Pup Bread recipe, meaning it's made mostly of eggs, providing a light and low-carb twist on this Italian and American classic. For sauce, we use our beet-and-sweet-potato-based Ketchpup. Use any toppings of your choice, but Ced and Edith love beef, bell peppers, mushrooms, chicken, pork, squash, and sardines.

Pupza Crust

3 egg whites (about 90 g)

1 egg yolk

1 heaping tbsp (10 g) coconut flour

¼ cup (50 g) Ketchpup (page 181)

Topping Ideas

(choose as many as you like)

¼ oz (7 g) freeze-dried beef liver

½ oz (15 g) ground beef, cooked

1 button or cremini mushroom, sliced and cooked

5 small pineapple slices

3 tbsp (15 g) shredded mozzarella and/or goat cheese (about 1 tbsp per pizza)

Basil leaves, for garnish

Other topping ideas: thinly sliced bell peppers, chopped spinach, sardines, organ meats

Ranch Dressing
(optional)

1 ounce (30 ml) kefir or plain Greek yogurt

Handful of herbs (dill, basil, etc.)

1. Make the crust: Preheat the oven to 325°F (165°C). Line a baking sheet with parchment paper.

2. Whisk the egg whites in a bowl until stiff peaks form. This means the egg becomes thick and shiny and when you remove the whisk a "peak" is left behind and stands up on its own. It may take up to 5 minutes with an electric mixer.

3. Using a spatula, gently fold in the egg yolk and coconut flour.

4. Scoop three dollops of the mixture onto the prepared baking sheet and use a spoon to shape each into a circle. Add more around the edges (piping works well here) to form a raised crust. *Trust the process!* It looks like mashed potatoes right now, but it will work out.

5. Bake for about 15–20 minutes, or until the crusts are set and golden brown.

6. Add toppings: Spread a thin layer of Ketchpup on each crust as sauce and add your toppings.

7. Optionally, heat the oven to broil. Broil for 2–3 minutes to melt the cheese.

8. Let the Pupzas cool, slice into bite-sized pieces safe for your dog, and serve.

Enchiladogs Verdes

MAKES 6 ENCHILADOGS, 850 CALORIES

Here's a traditional Mexican dish made with a canine twist. You can use premade corn tortillas, but if you—and your dog—happen to love quinoa, this homemade variety is pretty cool. The filling can be made with any meat, and if you want a red Enchiladog sauce, substitute Ketchpup (page 181).

Quinoa Tortillas

½ cup (95 g) dry quinoa

1 cup (240 ml) water

1 tsp (5 g) coconut oil, tallow, butter, or other oil, for cooking

Enchiladog filling

½ lb (227 g) boneless chicken breast or thighs

Salsa

1 (120 g) green bell pepper, stem and seeds removed

2 oz (60 g) broccoli florets

Optional Toppings

1 oz (30 g) cheese of choice (we use goat mozzarella)

1 oz (30 g) plain yogurt

Pinch of chopped cilantro

Quinoa Tortillas

1. Soak the dry quinoa for 3 hours (or overnight in the fridge) in a bowl of cool water.

2. Drain the quinoa and transfer to a blender. Purée with 1 cup (240 ml) fresh water until you have a pancake batter consistency.

3. Heat a flat, nonstick pan on medium heat. Melt the oil, tallow, or butter and swirl to coat the pan. Pour some of the batter onto the pan and use a spatula or crepe stick to spread it out into a circle. Cook for 1–2 minutes on each side, or until lightly browned. Repeat with the remaining batter. Keep the finished Quinoa Tortillas under a tea towel so they don't dry out.

Enchiladogs

1. Place the chicken in a pot and add enough water to cover. Bring to a boil on medium-high, reduce the heat to low, and simmer for 15–20 minutes, or until the chicken is cooked through. Remove the chicken and shred it. Keep the broth in the pot.

2. To make the salsa, use the same pot with the leftover chicken broth and boil the bell pepper and broccoli until soft, 8–10 minutes.

3. Transfer the cooked vegetables to a blender. Add about ½ cup (120 ml) of the chicken broth and blend into a sauce. Add more broth until you reach your desired consistency.

4. To assemble the Enchiladogs, place some shredded chicken inside each tortilla and roll. Cover the tortillas in a generous amount of the salsa. Optionally, top with shredded cheese, yogurt, and cilantro. Cool completely before serving. Store any leftover portions in airtight containers in the fridge for up to 4 days.

PUP "FRIED" CHICKEN

"Fried" Chicken

MAKES 800 CALORIES

Fried chicken is one of those irresistibly tasty meals that dogs unfortunately have to miss out on. Fast food, being made up of highly processed ingredients, just isn't good for them. But as with all people foods, we have a doggified alternative that you can feel good about giving them.

½ lb (227 g) boneless, skinless chicken thighs

1 egg

¼ cup (25 g) coconut flour

½ cup (60 g) wheat germ, hemp seeds, rolled oats, or cooked quinoa (you choose!)

1. Preheat the oven to 400°F (205°C).

2. Cut the chicken into small, bite-sized pieces.

3. Prepare three bowls for your dredging station: Whisk the egg in one bowl. Put the coconut flour in another. Finally, have the wheat germ, hemp seeds, oats, or cooked quinoa ready in another bowl—this will be your crumb coating.

4. Dip each piece of chicken in the coconut flour, then the egg, and then your choice of crumb. After dipping, place each chicken piece on a rimmed baking sheet.

5. Bake for 15–20 minutes, or until cooked through and golden brown.

6. Cool completely before portioning and serving. Make sure your dog has a drink to pair with their meal! Store leftovers in the fridge for up to 4 days.

Note: If you have an air fryer, you can air fry your "Fried" Chicken for extra crunch and appeal.

In a pinch, skip making a dough and use store-bought wonton wrappers. Just double-check the ingredients to make sure they are dog friendly.

Dim Sum Duo—Cheung Fur and Siu Paw

Dim sum, a traditional Chinese meal of small plates, is a dining experience that everyone has to try at least once. It's so much fun and will fill you up with its endless options. For the dogs, we've chosen just two iconic dishes—cheung fun (rice noodle rolls) and siu mai (steamed dumplings)—and made them into healthier versions for our pups.

Cheung Fur

MAKES 6 CHEUNG FURS, 200 CALORIES

6 napa cabbage leaves
¼ lb (114 g) ground turkey
½ tsp sesame seeds

---

1. Fill a steamer pot with water and bring to a boil over medium-high heat. Blanch the napa cabbage leaves in the boiling water for 1 minute. Remove them with a slotted spoon and set aside. Keep the water boiling.

2. Add some of the ground turkey to each leaf and roll vertically (burrito style).

3. Arrange the rolled leaves in a steamer basket and steam over a rolling boil for 8–10 minutes, until turkey is cooked through.

4. Sprinkle with sesame seeds. Cool completely before serving.

Siu Paw

MAKES 10 SIU PAWS, 600 CALORIES

1 egg
⅔ cup (60 g) chickpea flour or oat flour, plus more as needed
¼ lb (114 g) ground turkey
1 tsp (4g) salmon roe (optional)

---

1. In a small bowl, combine the egg with the chickpea flour to form a dough. Add more flour as needed. If the dough is dry, add a splash of water.

2. Roll the dough out on a floured surface, or between two sheets of parchment paper, until paper thin. (Depending on how thick you roll the dough, you may have leftovers, which you can cut and cook like Pawsta [page 197] and/or freeze for later).

3. Use 2- to 3-inch (6- to 9-cm) round cookie cutters to cut out circles.

4. Place 1 tbsp (15 g) of the ground meat in the center of each circle and bring the edges up to wrap around. Place the dumplings in a steamer basket.

5. Fill a steamer pot with water and bring to a boil over medium-high heat. Steam the dumplings over a rolling boil for 10–12 minutes.

6. Optionally, top with salmon roe. Cool completely before serving.

Special Occasions and Holidays

Got a special day coming up on the calendar? Don't leave your pup eating regular chow while the rest of the family gets the good stuff. Whether it's a holiday, your dog's birthday, or the right time for a fun activity, these recipes will help you make a treat that's both enjoyable and safe!

Why do we bring up safety? Every year around the holidays, there is a spike in emergency room visits for both people and pets. Celebration and family time make moderation difficult. Rather than taking risks by feeding your pups heavily seasoned foods they aren't used to, or worse, depriving them so they resort to rummaging through the trash, you can serve these special meals to them.

These recipes are more involved but still include a range of simple to advanced options. No matter your skill level, you will be able to spoil your pet with these recipes.

Sunday Rufflade

GRAIN-FREE 🐾 MAKES 2,950 CALORIES

After a hard week of work protecting your home from intruders, fending off the vacuum cleaner, and inspecting your groceries for poison, your pup deserves a fancy meal. Make them this low-carb roast dinner, inspired by beef roulade, that's not only stunning but nutritious, too. Serve as the centerpiece dish at your dinner pawrty, or make it for one! Simply slice and freeze leftovers for later. If you don't feel confident in your butchering skills, use a long piece of flank steak—it's already thin and ready to roll. Note that you will need butcher's twine to tie your Rufflade.

1 tbsp (15 g) coconut oil

2 cups (120 g) chopped kale

1 medium (4 oz / 120 g) carrot, diced

2 lb (908 g) cross rib roast, rump roast, or flank steak

⅓ cup (40 g) hemp seeds

2 cups (227 g) butternut squash chunks

1. In a large pan, melt the coconut oil on medium-low. Sauté the kale and carrot for 8–10 minutes, or until most of the moisture has evaporated.

2. Preheat the oven to 350°F (175°C).

3. Place the roast on a cutting board. Cut horizontally through the middle of the meat, parallel to the cutting board, stopping before you slice all the way through. This cut is similar to a butterfly, except thinner and longer. You should end up with one long, thin slab, about 1 inch thick. If you are using a piece of flank steak, you can hammer it with a meat tenderizer to further thin it out.

4. Spread the kale and carrot mixture over the meat, then evenly sprinkle on the hemp seeds.

5. Roll the beef into a tight spiral, and secure with at least three strands of butcher's twine, evenly spaced along the roll.

6. Place the roast into a baking dish with a lid or Dutch oven and surround the beef with the butternut squash cubes.

7. Cover and bake for 1 hour to 1 hour and 15 minutes, checking the internal temperature of the roast with a meat thermometer after 1 hour. The roast is done when the temperature has reached 135°F (57°C; medium-rare). Let it rest for 15 minutes, then remove the twine and carve into slices.

8. Chop into appropriate bite sizes for your dog before serving. Plate with pieces of roasted squash and cool before serving. Store any leftover portions in airtight containers in the fridge for up to 4 days.

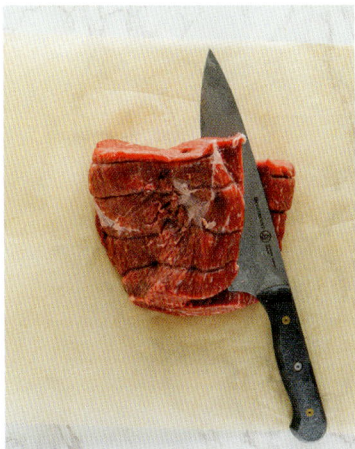
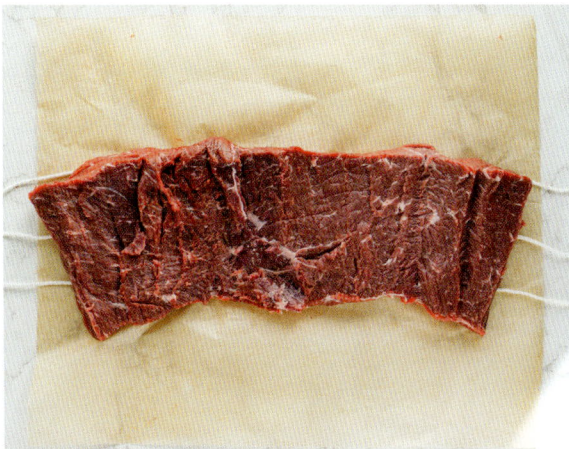

Tip: If your cake comes out a little dry, brush each layer with goat milk, bone broth, or water before frosting. This moistens and softens the cake, making it even more enjoyable for your dog, as well as safer for those speedy and less careful eaters.

Frosted Layer Cake

MAKES 1 CAKE, 625 CALORIES WITHOUT ADDITIONAL TOPPINGS

Whether you're throwing a huge pawrty or just want to bake a cake on a Monday, your dog will appreciate this recipe made with love. Do we need a special reason to celebrate, after all?

This recipe fills two 4-inch (10 cm) cake pans (for a very tall cake) or two 6-inch (15 cm) cake pans (for a shorter cake). For the frosting, look for a plain, strained Greek yogurt. (Dairy sensitivity? Try a plain coconut yogurt!)

When it comes to toppings, let your creativity shine. Top with your choice of dog-friendly fruits such as fresh or freeze-dried strawberries, blueberries, raspberries, blackberries, mango chunks, or banana slices; or "sprinkles" of hemp hearts, crushed pumpkin seeds, bee pollen, or coconut flakes. A simple dusting of carob or goat milk powder looks beautiful, too.

For Yellow Cake

4 large eggs

½ cup (50 g) oat flour

2 tbsp (30 g) melted coconut oil, melted beef tallow, or olive oil

For Carob Cake

4 large eggs

⅓ cup (40 g) oat flour

¼ cup (20 g) carob powder

2 tbsp (30 g) melted coconut oil, melted beef tallow, or olive oil

Frosting

1 cup (240 g) plain Greek yogurt

1 tsp (3 g) carob powder, crushed freeze-dried strawberries, pumpkin powder, or crushed freeze-dried beef liver

1. Preheat your oven to 350°F (175°C). Cut two circles from parchment paper to fit the bottoms of two 4- or 6-inch (10- or 15-cm) cake pans. Line the pans with the paper.

2. In a large bowl with a hand mixer, or in a stand mixer with a wire whip attachment, whisk the eggs on high speed for 4–5 minutes, or until tripled in size, pale yellow, and fluffy.

3. Sift in the oat flour (for yellow cake) or oat flour and carob powder (for carob cake), drizzle in the oil or tallow, and fold together gently with a spatula.

4. Gently divide the batter into the prepared cake pans.

5. Bake for 18–20 minutes, or until the cakes have puffed up and the centers have set (give them a wiggle; they will be very jiggly if they're not yet done).

6. Allow the cakes to cool completely before removing from the pans.

7. To make the frosting, combine the yogurt with your choice of flavor powder in a small bowl. Frost one layer (you can also add some toppings here, if you like), then sandwich the second layer on top and frost the top and sides. Decorate with toppings or piped frosting if you wish.

8. Slice the cake and delight your pup! Don't forget to serve in appropriate bite sizes for your pup. The excitement of a giant cake can lead to overzealous chomping. Refrigerate any leftover cake in airtight containers for up to 3 days, or freeze individual slices for up to 6 months.

Lunar New Year Spring Rolls

MAKES 6-8 ROLLS, 600 CALORIES

Usually eaten around the Spring Festival in China, spring rolls are a great appetizer for any occasion. These dog-friendly rolls can be made with any protein, but we like ground pork mixed with carrots, mushrooms, and cabbage. You can use regular store-bought spring roll wrappers, or rice paper for a gluten-free option. Check the label to make sure your wrappers are made from minimal, dog-friendly ingredients. Instead of deep-frying, coat the egg rolls lightly in egg wash and bake. They come out crunchy and tasty enough that you may want to enjoy one yourself.

¼ lb (114 g) ground pork

2 (2½ oz / 70 g) napa cabbage leaves, finely chopped

4 small (2 oz / 50 g) shiitake mushrooms, finely chopped

1 small (2 oz / 50 g) carrot, finely chopped

1 large egg

3–4 sheets spring roll/ egg roll wrappers or rice paper wrappers, cut in half

G'boy Sauce
(for dipping)

¼ cup (60 ml) dog-friendly broth

¼ tsp (0.5 g) carob powder

1. Heat a large frying pan or wok on medium heat. Cook the pork, cabbage, mushrooms, and carrot, stirring and breaking up the pork, until the meat is cooked through and the liquid has released and evaporated from the veggies, 5–8 minutes. Drain the excess liquid. Set aside to cool completely before filling the rolls.

2. Preheat the oven to 350°F (175°C). Line a baking sheet with parchment paper.

3. Beat the egg in a small bowl to make the egg wash.

4. Place one wrapper on your work surface with one corner pointing toward you. If using rice paper wrappers, dip quickly into a shallow bowl of water to soften.

5. Place about 2 tbsp (60 g) of the pork and veggie mixture onto the wrapper, about one-third of the way up from the bottom corner. (Don't overfill as the roll will be hard to seal.)

6. Fold the bottom corner up over the filling, tuck the side corners in, and roll almost all the way up.

7. At the top corner, add a dab of egg wash to seal the egg roll, then continue rolling until the wrapper is completely sealed. Place the roll on the prepared baking sheet.

8. Repeat until all the filling has been used. You should end up with 6–8 rolls (you'll have extra wrappers left over, which you can use to make some egg rolls for yourself!).

9. Brush the rolls with the egg wash.

10. Bake for about 20 minutes (or air fry at 350°F / 175°C for 10 minutes), or just until golden brown.

Recipe continues . . .

11. Let the rolls cool completely before serving. Serve in appropriate bite sizes. Don't forget to dip the rolls in some G'boy Sauce! Store any leftover portions in airtight containers in the fridge for up to 4 days.

Christmas Morning Pup Cocoa and Marshmallows

GRAIN-FREE 🐾 **MAKES 250 CALORIES**

Who would've thought you could make marshmallows for dogs? These have the same fluffy look and feel, without any of the sugar. They work almost as well as regular marshmallows, meaning you can lightly toast them!

Marshmallows

1 tbsp (10 g) plain gelatin powder

½ cup (120 ml) cold water, divided in half

2 egg whites

1 tbsp (10 g) goat milk powder, for dusting (optional)

Pup Cocoa

1 cup (240 ml) goat milk (if using powdered goat milk, follow the package directions to rehydrate)

½ tsp (1 g) carob powder

1. Line an 8 × 4-inch (20 × 10 cm) or other small loaf pan with plastic wrap or parchment paper.

2. In a bowl, whisk the gelatin powder with ¼ cup (60 ml) of the cold water. Give the gelatin about 5 minutes to bloom, or absorb the water.

3. Meanwhile, in another bowl with a hand mixer, or in a stand mixer with a wire whip attachment, whisk the egg whites until stiff peaks form and the eggs become shiny. This may take 4–5 minutes of high-speed whisking.

4. Bring the remaining ¼ cup (60 ml) water to a boil. Remove the water from the heat for 30 seconds, then add it to the bloomed gelatin. Stir until the lumps are dissolved.

5. With the mixer on medium speed, slowly drizzle the liquid gelatin into the egg whites. The mixture will thin out at first, but keep mixing on high and it will thicken again. Mix for 1–2 minutes.

6. Pour the mixture into the prepared pan. Cover with plastic wrap or parchment paper. Refrigerate for at least 3 hours, or until set.

7. Turn the marshmallow slab out onto a clean work surface. Slice into cubes. Optionally, dust with the goat milk powder. Keep the marshmallows in an airtight container in the fridge for up to 3 days.

8. When you're ready to make the cocoa, gently heat the goat milk in a small pot over low heat to 100°F (40°C), then whisk in the carob powder. Transfer to your dog's drinking dish, cool, top with a fresh marshmallow, and serve.

Tip: Prep the marshmallows a day before so that they are ready to go on Christmas Day.

gelatin

egg whites

Pawlentine's Barkuterie

This adogable Barkuterie board features an array of dog-friendly fruits, cheeses, oysters, and heart-shaped cookies based on our Cereal Cookie recipe (page 256)—plus Carob-Covered Strawberries for your pup to share with their Pawlentine's date!

Carob-Covered Strawberries

MAKES 325 CALORIES

10 small (3½ oz / 100 g) strawberries
2 tbsp (30 g) coconut oil
1 heaping tbsp (10 g) carob powder

---

1. Wash and dry the strawberries. Place them in the freezer while you do the next step.

2. In a small pan or pot on low heat, melt together the coconut oil and carob powder. Stir until fully combined. Remove from the heat.

3. Pour the melted mixture into a small bowl or espresso cup (it's the perfect shape and size for dipping). Allow the carob mixture to cool for about 5 minutes before you start. If it's too warm, it will melt right off the strawberries.

4. Take the cold strawberries and dip them into the carob mixture, wiping the excess off on the edge of the bowl. The carob should harden quickly on the cold strawberries, but you can pop them in the freezer for another 10 minutes to let them set.

5. Feed 1–2 strawberries per 10 lb (4.5 kg) of your dog's weight. Use your best judgment depending on how big the strawberry is. Slice each strawberry into smaller pieces for smaller dogs and fast eaters, as whole strawberries can be a choking hazard. Keep in the fridge for up to 2 days, or freeze for up to 6 months.

Barkuterie Board

MAKES 400 CALORIES

2 small slices (1 oz / 30 g) cheese of choice (mozzarella, goat cheese, Brie, Comté, Gruyère)
Handful (1 oz / 30 g) of fruits of choice (blueberries, raspberries, blackberries, pineapple, apple)
6 Carob-Covered Strawberries (see preceding recipe)
Handful (1 oz / 30 g) of seafood (freeze-dried or canned oysters, mussels, sardines, mackerel)
Handful (1 oz / 30 g) of heart cookies (base recipe on Cereal Cookies, page 256)

---

1. Assemble the board with 3–6 pieces of each ingredient.

2. Though loading the board up is great for a photo op, we would suggest limiting actual feeding to 2 small pieces of each item per 10 lb (4.5 kg) of your dog's weight.

3. Make sure to cut up all ingredients to the best size for your pup to eat.

If you can't find seafood canned in water, simply go for seafood canned in olive oil. Just dab the pieces on a paper towel to remove excess oil. Go for plain, and avoid any that are flavored with spices.

Moon Festival Mooncakes

MAKES 3 MOONCAKES, 850 CALORIES

These sweet treats are enjoyed during the Mid-Autumn Festival in China. The round shape symbolizes the moon, and they are filled with various kinds of delicacies ranging from sweet beans to salted meats. Why limit the fun to just your human family? Our doggo mooncakes are crafted with two varieties of sweet potatoes, coconut oil, and egg yolks. You will need mooncake molds, which you can easily find online.

3 egg yolks

1 small (8.5 oz / 240 g) orange sweet potato, peeled and cubed

1 small (8.5 oz / 240 g) purple sweet potato, peeled and cubed

1 cup (100 g) oat flour

1 tsp (5 g) coconut oil

1. Preheat the oven to 325°F (165°C). Line a small rimmed baking sheet with parchment paper.

2. Place the egg yolks on the prepared baking sheet. Bake until they're solid, 10–15 minutes. Check on them often—as soon as they turn solid, take them out of the oven and set aside (keep the parchment paper).

3. Meanwhile, bring a pot of water to a boil over medium-high heat. Add the sweet potatoes and boil for about 10 minutes, or until they can be easily pierced with a fork. Strain and let cool slightly.

4. Transfer the orange sweet potato to a large bowl. Slowly add a small amount of oat flour at a time, mashing and mixing until a dough forms. You may end up using less than the full amount of flour. When you have a dough that you can shape with your hands without much sticking, it's just right!

5. Mash the purple sweet potato in another bowl.

6. Taking into account the size of your mooncake molds, form a small ball with the purple potato and flatten. Place one baked egg yolk in this flattened ball and encase it, forming a ball.

7. Wrap the purple ball in a thin layer of the orange potato dough. Keep in mind that you need the ball to be able to fit snugly in the mooncake mold.

8. Repeat until you have wrapped all the egg yolks in two layers of sweet potato. Generously grease the balls with the coconut oil (this will help you release them from the mooncake molds).

9. Place a ball in a mooncake mold and press it down firmly onto the parchment-lined baking sheet. Lift and push the mooncake out of the mold. Repeat with the other cakes.

10. Bake for 20–25 minutes, or until the outer layer is set.

11. Cool the mooncakes before slicing into bite-sized pieces and serving. Store any leftovers in an airtight container in the fridge for up to 4 days.

Howloween Dogviled Eggs

GRAIN-FREE ❧ MAKES 275 CALORIES

This treat may look spooky, but you have nothing to fear. Eggs are one of the most nutritious foods for pups and people alike, and the antioxidants in this "eyeball" are the blueberry on top, literally!

3 large eggs

2 tbsp (30 g) plain Greek yogurt

¼ cup (50 g) cooked vegetables of choice (such as peas or beets)

6 blueberries

1. Bring a pot of water to a boil over medium heat. With a spoon or skimmer, gently lower in the eggs. Cook for 10 minutes. Meanwhile, prepare an ice bath.

2. Transfer the eggs to the ice bath to cool.

3. Peel the eggs and slice them in half lengthwise. Transfer the yolks to a separate bowl. Place the white halves on a plate.

4. Use a fork or mortar and pestle to mash the yolks with the yogurt and veggies. For a smoother mix, use a blender.

5. Spoon (or pipe with a piping bag) the mixture back into the egg halves.

6. Top each egg with a blueberry.

7. Serve appropriate portions for your pup (about 1 whole egg per 10 lb / 4.5 kg of your dog's weight). Store any leftovers in an airtight container in the fridge for up to 3 days.

Healthy Holiday Platter

GRAIN-FREE ❧ MAKES 500 CALORIES

During the Thanksgiving and Christmas season, a lot of cooking happens, and all the smells of food in the kitchen have to be driving your dog crazy. We don't want to make even more work for you, so here's an easy one-plate holidog meal made up from bits and bobs you'll likely already have on hand. It all steams together into one nice, juicy meal. Your pup will have their own festive dinner and can avoid eating table scraps of foods with ingredients that don't serve them well.

¼ lb (114 g) chicken or turkey breast

3–6 chicken hearts (optional)

¼ cup (60 g) green beans

½ small (120 g) sweet potato, thinly sliced

Pinch of ground turmeric (optional)

1 sprig thyme or rosemary (optional)

1 tbsp (15 g) olive oil

1. Fill a steamer pot with water and bring to a boil over medium-high heat.

2. On a heatproof plate, arrange the chicken or turkey breast, chicken hearts (if using), green beans, and sweet potato. Optionally, sprinkle turmeric over the meat and top with a sprig of thyme or rosemary.

3. Steam the meat and veggies over a rolling boil for 20–25 minutes, or until the meat is cooked through (reaches an internal temperature of 165°F / 75°C).

4. Remove and discard the thyme or rosemary (if using). Shred or slice the meat and veggies into bite-sized pieces. Cool completely before portioning and serving. Drizzle with the olive oil and serve with the juices. Store any leftovers in airtight containers in the fridge for up to 4 days.

Pupkin Pie Jellies

GRAIN-FREE ❧ MAKES 250 CALORIES

What holiday dinner is complete without a pumpkin pie? These Pupkin Pie Jellies will make your dog's day and only take 15 minutes out of yours. They're also sneakily healthy as they're full of fiber from the pumpkin and protein from the gelatin.

½ cup (120 ml) water, divided

1½ tbsp (15 g) plain gelatin powder

1 (15 oz / 425 g) can plain pumpkin puree

Small pinch of Ceylon cinnamon, ground turmeric, and/or ground ginger (optional)

¼ cup (60 g) plain Greek yogurt, for garnish

1. In a small bowl, combine ¼ cup (60 ml) of the water with the gelatin powder. Stir and let the gelatin absorb the water. This is called "letting the gelatin bloom." It will turn into a solid disc and this is fine!

2. Meanwhile, in a pot over medium heat, heat the pumpkin puree with the remaining ¼ cup (60 ml) water until the pumpkin starts to bubble. Stir in any optional spices and remove from the heat. Let it cool for 30 seconds.

3. Add the bloomed gelatin to the still-hot pumpkin puree and stir until completely dissolved.

4. Transfer the mixture to an 8-inch (20-cm) square pan (or a festive silicone mold). Refrigerate for at least 3 hours, or until set.

5. Turn the gelatin out onto a cutting board and slice into pieces (long triangles make the jellies look just like pieces of pumpkin pie). Serve with a dollop of yogurt on top for a final touch. Store leftover portions in an airtight container in the refrigerator for up to 4 days.

Note: To add flavor and make these even more appealing for pickier dogs, use a dog-friendly broth or goat milk instead of water. Keep in mind that this will add calories.

Bark Wellington with Sweet Potato Mash and Gravy

MAKES 1,000 CALORIES

When there's something big to celebrate, this is the dish to make. Taking inspiration from the riff on beef Wellington made famous by chef Gordon Ramsay, we keep the main construction techniques but swap out some of the ingredients for dog-friendly ones.

Filling

1 large (3 oz / 90 g) carrot

About 15 large (10 oz / 300 g) cremini mushrooms

Tallow or coconut oil, for searing

10 oz (200–300 g) lean steak of choice

Sprinkle of ground turmeric (optional)

Dough

⅔ cup (70 g) oat flour, plus more as needed and for rolling

2 tbsp (30 g) coconut oil

2–3 tbsp (30 ml) cold water

1 egg (optional, for egg wash)

Gravy

½ cup (120 ml) dog-friendly broth, at room temperature

¼ tsp (1 g) tapioca starch, plus more as needed

Pinch of carob powder (optional)

Sides

½ cup (60 g) cubed sweet potato or cauliflower florets

¼ cup (40 g) frozen peas

Prep

1. Use a vegetable peeler to vertically peel the carrot into thin ribbons.

2. Bring a small pot of water to a boil over medium heat and blanch the carrot ribbons for 1 minute. Remove them from the water with a slotted spoon and set aside. This softens the carrot ribbons so that they can bend without breaking.

3. Finely chop the mushrooms, or pulse in a food processor until a fine crumb is achieved. Set aside.

Steak and Mushroom Duxelles

1. Heat a medium pan over medium-high heat. Coat with a little bit of tallow or coconut oil. Sear the steak for 30 seconds on each side. The inside should still be very rare. Remove the steak and set aside.

2. Optionally, coat the steak in a dusting of turmeric.

3. In the pan used to sear the steak, cook the finely chopped mushrooms over medium-low heat for 10–15 minutes, or until the mushrooms are thoroughly cooked and all the liquid has evaporated. Remove the pan from the heat and allow the mushroom duxelles to cool.

> Note: May we suggest a glass of Bourdog (page 285) to pair with the Bark Wellington?

Assemble the Filling

Assemble the Filling

1. Place a layer of plastic wrap over your work surface. Assemble the carrot strips into a sheet large enough to fully wrap around the piece of steak.

2. Spread the mushroom duxelles in a layer on the carrot sheet.

3. Place the steak on top.

4. Using the plastic wrap, bring the ends of the carrot up and over the steak to encase it; roll and wrap tightly. Twist the ends of the plastic wrap to seal it all together. Place in the fridge while you make the dough.

Make the Dough

Make the Dough

1. In a mixing bowl, crumble together the oat flour and coconut oil until you have a rough, crumbly texture.

2. Add the water and mix until a soft dough forms. It should be soft enough to roll out. Add more water or oat flour as needed.

3. Tip the dough out onto a work surface dusted with more oat flour, or onto parchment paper. Roll the dough out until it's thin (1⁄16 inch / 1.5 mm) and large enough to wrap around the filling.

Assemble the Wellington

Assemble the Wellington

1. Preheat the oven to 415°F (212°C).

2. Remove the filling from the plastic wrap and place it on the dough. Fold the dough tightly over the steak and pinch at the ends to seal. Transfer the Bark Wellington to a baking sheet lined with parchment paper.

3. Optionally, whisk the egg, then brush the Bark Wellington on all sides with egg. For extra flair, gently score lines using the back of a knife.

4. Bake for 20–30 minutes, or until the crust is golden and an internal temperature of 135°F (57°C) is reached for a medium-rare cook.

5. While the Bark Wellington bakes, prep your sides.

Gravy

1. In a small saucepan on low heat, whisk the broth with the tapioca starch and bring to a simmer.

2. Stir the broth mixture until it thickens to a gravy-like consistency. Optionally, add a pinch of carob powder for color. If the gravy is too thick, add a splash of water. If it's too thin, combine another ¼ tsp (1 g) tapioca starch with 2 tbsp (30 ml) water in a small bowl, pour the mixture into the gravy, and whisk until the gravy thickens.

Mash

1. Boil or steam the sweet potato or cauliflower until very soft, about 10 minutes.

2. Pulse the sweet potato in a blender or simply mash with a fork.

3. Use the same water to boil peas for 5 minutes.

Serve

Let the Bark Wellington rest for at least 10 minutes before slicing. Plate the Wellington, mash, peas, and gravy, chop into bite-sized pieces, and cool all food before serving. Store leftover portions in an airtight container in the refrigerator for up to 4 days.

Tip: Picky pup? Add a small knob of unsalted butter or splash of goat milk to your mash to make it more enticing.

233

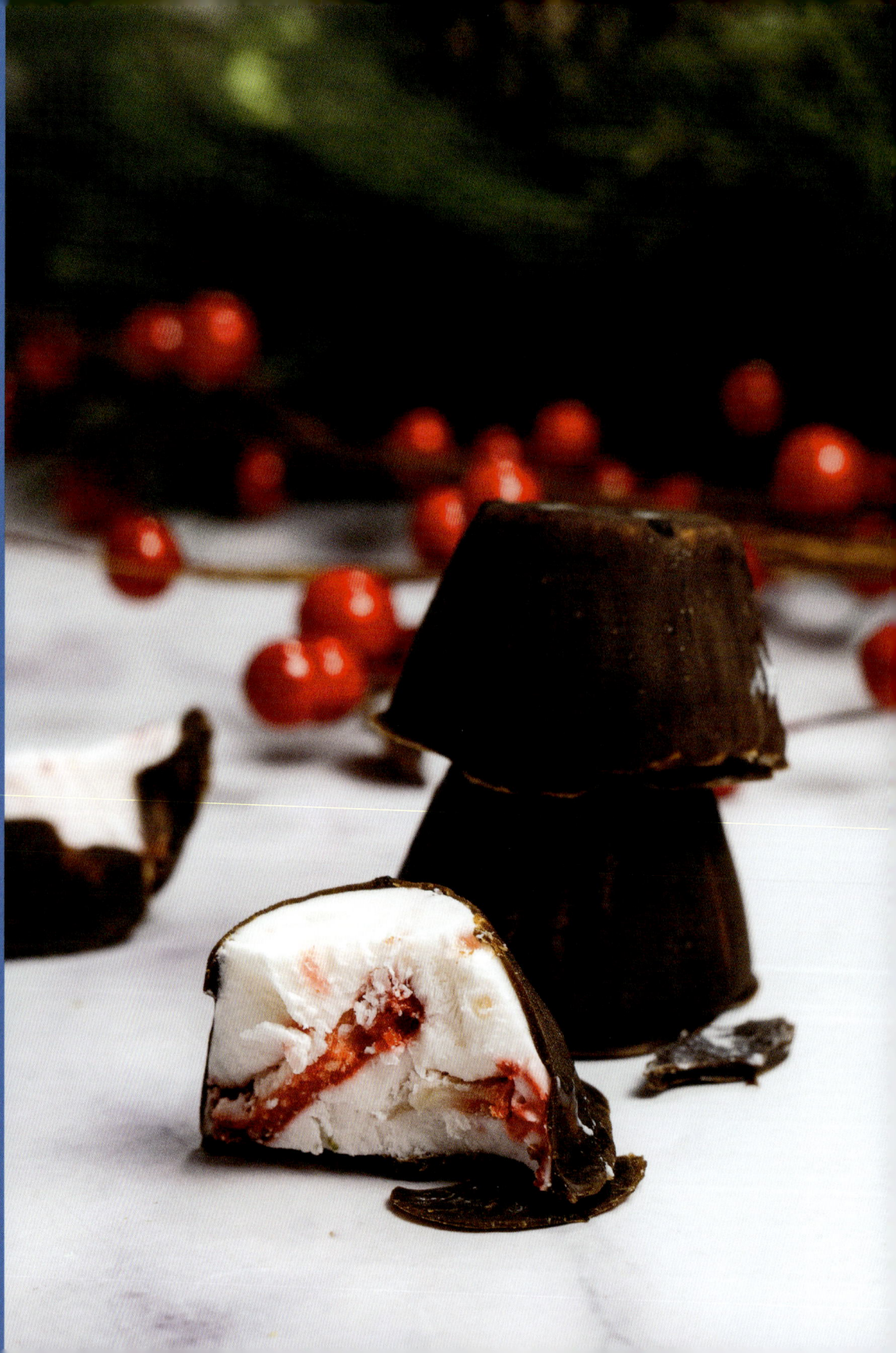

Puppermint Patties

GRAIN-FREE 🐾 **MAKES 20 SMALL PATTIES, 600 CALORIES**

Peppermint patties are often enjoyed during the holidays, but these Puppermint Patties can be enjoyed year-round. Because they are frozen, your pup will probably love them on a hot summer day, too. You don't need silicone molds to make these, but they are recommended.

Handful of fresh or freeze-dried berries

A few sprigs of mint

1 cup (240 g) plain Greek yogurt

¼ cup (50 g) coconut oil

2 tbsp (30 g) carob powder

1. Crush the berries slightly. Remove the leaves from the mint sprigs and finely chop or crush them. Discard the stems.

2. Stir together the yogurt, berries, and mint in a bowl.

3. Spoon the mixture into silicone molds. If you don't have silicone molds, spoon small dollops onto parchment paper and smooth them down into discs. Freeze for 3 hours, or until set.

4. When you're ready to make the shell, line a rimmed baking sheet with parchment paper.

5. Melt the coconut oil over low heat in a saucepan, then remove from heat and whisk in the carob powder. Let the carob–coconut oil mixture cool for 5–10 minutes before dipping.

6. Remove the frozen yogurt pieces from the molds. Dip the frozen yogurt bits into the carob–coconut oil mixture to coat, and place them on the baking sheet.

7. Freeze again for at least 30 minutes.

8. Transfer the frozen treats to a plastic bag or container and keep frozen for up to six months until you're ready to serve.

Christmas Eve Pawrogis

MAKES 825 CALORIES

Pierogies are Polish dumplings enjoyed in the winter months and as a part of Christmas Eve dinner. Cedric and Edith love trying foods from around the world, and these Pawrogis might be at the top of their list. Traditional fillings range from potatoes and cheese to mushrooms and sauerkraut. We're keeping it simple so you can whip these up in no time, but feel free to be adventurous and come up with your own fillings.

Filling
¼ lb (114 g) ground beef

Dough
1 large egg

1 cup (100 g) oat flour, plus more as needed and for rolling

1 tbsp (15 ml) olive oil

Garnish and Sides
1 tbsp (5 g) kefir, for drizzling

1 tbsp (4 g) chopped fresh dill

1 tbsp (8 g) cooked chopped beets or 1 tbsp (10 g) plain sauerkraut (optional)

Filling

1. In a small pan over medium heat, brown the ground beef.

2. Transfer the beef to a food processor or blender and pulse until it forms a paste. Add a splash of water if needed to help the beef blend. (This step is optional, but makes the filling easier to work with.)

Dough

1. In a bowl, combine the egg, oat flour, and olive oil to form a dough.

2. On a floured surface, roll the dough out into a thin slab. Use circle cookie cutters to cut out circles (about 3 inches/8 cm in diameter).

Wrap

1. Add about 1 tbsp (15 g) of the ground beef paste to the center of each Pawrogi wrapper.

2. Fold each wrapper in half and press the sides together firmly.

3. Use a fork to press down along the edges for a secure seal and nice pattern.

Cook and Plate

1. Bring a pot of water to a boil over medium-high heat.

2. Gently spoon in the Pawrogis and boil for 5–6 minutes.

3. Remove with a slotted spoon.

4. Arrange the Pawrogis on a plate and top with a drizzle of kefir and a sprinkle of fresh dill.

5. If using, serve with a small side of cooked beets or sauerkraut (yes, dogs can have sauerkraut!). Cool completely before serving. Store leftover portions in an airtight container in the refrigerator for up to 4 days.

Wrap

New Year's Eve Pawquettes and Shrimp Dogtail

These cheesy Pawquettes and shrimp with Pawrinara sauce (see Ketchpup recipe, page 181) make the perfect hors d'oeuvres—or hors d'ogoeuvres (if you dare)—for a special occasion. While the Pawquettes take a little bit of work to make, the cheese pull is worth it. The Shrimp Dogtail, although as simple as boiling shrimp, will stun your pawrtygoers! Serve alongside a glass of Champup (page 284) for a truly unforgettable New Year's Eve. (You know your pup will be waiting to give you a kiss when the clock strikes 12.)

Pawquettes

MAKES 10 PAWQUETTES, 600 CALORIES

1 small (8 ½ oz / 240 g) sweet potato, cooked and mashed
3 oz (85 g) block mozzarella cheese, cubed
½ cup (60 g) wheat germ

1. Preheat the oven to 425°F (220°C). Line a rimmed baking sheet with parchment paper.
2. Roll 2 heaping tbsp (20 g) of the mashed sweet potato into a ball and flatten it out. Add a cube of cheese in the center. Roll the sweet potato back up into a ball with the cheese secure in the center. Repeat with the remaining mashed sweet potato and cheese cubes.
3. Place the wheat germ in a small bowl. Roll each ball in the wheat germ to coat it, and place each ball on the prepared baking sheet.
4. Bake for 15 minutes, or until golden brown.
5. Cool completely before serving.

Shrimp Dogtail

MAKES 100 CALORIES

3 oz (90 g) peeled and deveined shrimp
¼ cup (60 g) Pawrinara sauce (use Ketchpup, page 181)

1. Bring a pot of water to a boil over medium heat and toss in the shrimp.
2. Meanwhile, prepare an ice bath.
3. Cook the shrimp for 3–4 minutes, or until they turn opaque and curl up into a C shape.
4. Transfer the shrimp to the ice bath to cool.
5. Serve with the Pawrinara sauce.

Breakfast and Brunch

Most days we just eat eggs for a quick breakfast prioritizing protein. But we can't deny our love for breakfast foods. Weekends and holiday mornings feature special treats like pancakes, waffles, and other breakfast delights. For our pups, these breakfast-themed treats are also meant to be enjoyed on special occasions, rather than for daily feeding.

Chia Seed Pawfait

GRAIN-FREE ❀ **MAKES 1 CUP (240 G) CHIA SEED PUDDING, 300 CALORIES (WITH COCONUT WATER, KEFIR, AND BERRIES)**

Chia seeds are full of fiber and plant protein, and they are even a good plant-based source of omega-3s. Combined with liquid, they turn into an all-natural pudding. Serve this up with layers of berries, your pup's favorite fruit, and perhaps some Dogranola (page 253).

1 cup (240 g) liquid (coconut water, water, or dog-friendly broth)

2 tbsp (30 g) kefir (optional)

3 tbsp (36 g) chia seeds

8–12 berries

1. In a bowl, combine the liquid, kefir (if using), and chia seeds. Stir well to ensure an even distribution of chia seeds.

2. Cover and refrigerate for at least 3 hours or overnight to allow the seeds to gel.

3. Serve the pudding with fresh berries or fruit of choice. As a suggestion, serve ¼ cup (about 50 g) pudding with 2–3 berries per 10 lb (4.5 kg) of your dog's weight. Store leftover portions in an airtight container in the refrigerator for up to 4 days.

Note: Soaking chia seeds before feeding is an important step. Never feed dry chia seeds!

243

Doggie Donuts

MAKES 9 SMALL DONUTS, 700 CALORIES WITH ALL OPTIONAL INGREDIENTS

Made with eggs and a bit of oat flour, these donuts may look temptingly like the real thing but are actually healthy treats. Whip up your choice of flavors: original glaze made with coconut oil and goat milk powder, dog-friendly chocolate icing made with carob powder, and even a strawberry glaze. Serve with Pup Cocoa (page 217) on a Saturday morning. Note that you'll need a donut pan for best results.

3 egg whites

3 tbsp (21 g) oat flour

1 egg yolk

3 tbsp (45 g) coconut oil, melted, plus more for greasing the pan

1 tsp (4 g) goat milk powder

1 tsp (3 g) carob powder (optional)

1 tbsp (8 g) crushed freeze-dried strawberries (optional)

1. Preheat the oven to 350°F (175°C). Grease a nonstick donut pan thoroughly with coconut oil.

2. In a large bowl with a hand mixer, whisk the egg whites on high speed until stiff peaks form. This may take up to 5 minutes. The egg whites should be extremely fluffy and thick.

3. Using a spatula, gently fold in the oat flour and egg yolk until just combined. Do not overmix. The mixture should still be light and airy.

4. Gently transfer the mixture to a piping bag or plastic bag.

5. Pipe the egg mixture into a nonstick donut pan. Overfill the molds slightly as the mixture will shrink a little in the oven.

6. Bake for 15–18 minutes, or until the donuts are golden brown.

7. Loosen the donuts from the mold and allow them to cool in the freezer while you prepare the glaze.

8. Melt the coconut oil on the stove in a saucepan or microwave in a microwave-safe bowl large enough to dip the donuts. Stir in the goat milk powder, and the carob or crushed strawberries (if using), until fully combined. Allow the glaze to cool to near room temperature before glazing for best results.

9. Dunk the chilled donuts into the glaze to coat lightly. Let them sit on a plate until the glaze hardens.

10. Break the donuts into small pieces for smaller dogs or dogs that eat too fast. Store in the fridge for up to 3 days—if they last that long!

Easiest Pupcakes

GRAIN-FREE 🐾 MAKES 5 MEDIUM PANCAKES, 350 CALORIES

You can share a healthy breakfast with your dog with these super easy two-ingredient pupcakes. These are a popular alternative to pancakes for people on low-carb diets, but because they are so quick to make from simple, dog-friendly ingredients, we think they work just as well for pups. If you want to add healthy toppings for your dog, try plain yogurt, hemp hearts, blueberries, local organic honey, and/or bee pollen.

1 banana or ½ cup (100 g) pumpkin or sweet potato puree

2 large eggs

1 tbsp (15 g) butter, for cooking, divided

1. Place the banana (or pumpkin or sweet potato, if using) and eggs in a blender and puree until smooth. If you don't have a blender handy, you can simply mash the banana well in a bowl, then thoroughly whisk in the eggs.

2. Melt half of the butter in a nonstick pan on medium heat.

3. Pour some of the batter into the pan in small circles (it will be runny, so no worries—it's not supposed to look like regular pancake batter).

4. Let the pancakes cook until almost set, 2–3 minutes, then flip and cook for another 30 seconds on the other side. Transfer to a plate. Repeat, using more butter to grease the pan as needed. You may need to make three or four batches depending on the size of the pancakes.

5. Cool the Pupcakes before serving. Store any leftovers in airtight containers in the fridge for up to 4 days.

Eggs Benedog

MAKES 2 EGGS BENEDOG, 375 CALORIES

A well-made eggs Benedict is the quintessential breakfast dish. Its many components make it a well-balanced and satisfying meal. Hollandaise sauce is the perfect combination of rich and tart flavor that can go with almost anything. Our pup version includes low-carb English muffins and a yogurt-based Hollandog Sauce to drizzle on top.

Muffins

2 large egg whites (save yolks for the sauce)

2 tbsp (14 g) oat flour

Drizzle of olive oil

Eggs Benedog

A few slices of zucchini

2 large eggs

Hollandog Sauce

2 egg yolks

1 tbsp (15 g) plain yogurt

Pinch of ground turmeric (optional)

Fresh dill, for garnish

1. In a bowl, using a hand blender, whisk the egg whites into stiff peaks. Gently fold in the oat flour.

2. Heat a drizzle of olive oil in a nonstick pan on medium heat. Spoon the egg white mixture into the pan in dollops, forming two patties. These will be your English muffins. Cook for 3–4 minutes on one side, or until browned and set underneath, then flip and cook another 2–3 minutes, or until browned and cooked through. Transfer the muffins to a plate.

3. In the same pan on medium heat, sauté the zucchini slices until softened, about 5 minutes. Remove from the heat.

4. Bring a small pot of water to a boil over medium heat, then turn the heat down to medium-low. (A low boil helps keep poached eggs intact.)

5. Crack the whole eggs directly into the water. Poach for 3–4 minutes. Gently stir the water to help the eggs form as they cook. Remove with a slotted spoon.

6. Place the uncooked egg yolks onto the slotted spoon and dunk them into the same pot of hot water for 10 seconds to gently pasteurize.

7. Whisk the yolks together with the yogurt and turmeric in a small bowl to make the Hollandog Sauce.

8. To assemble, top each muffin with half the zucchini slices and gently set a poached egg on top. Drizzle with the Hollandog Sauce and sprinkle with the fresh dill.

9. Cool the Eggs Benedog completely before serving to your dog. Don't forget to cut it up before serving to smaller dogs.

Sweet Potato Hash Barks

GRAIN-FREE 🐾 HYPOALLERGENIC 🐾 MAKES 340 CALORIES

Hash browns are a breakfast must-have (for us) and a great companion to any egg dish. These Hash Barks are made with sweet potatoes. Using sweet potatoes increases the vitamin A and fiber, which are both good for your pups. Since regular potatoes are in the nightshade family, they contain solanine that sweet potatoes (they're in the morning glory family) do not. While dogs can eat potatoes, they are more sensitive to solanine than people are. The flax or chia seeds helps bind the hash browns together.

1 tbsp (8 g) flaxseeds or chia seeds

3 tbsp (45 ml) water

1 medium (14.5 oz / 400 g) sweet potato, grated

1 heaping tbsp (18 g) coconut oil

1. Preheat the oven to 375°F (190°C) and line a rimmed baking sheet with parchment paper.

2. If using flaxseeds, roughly grind or crush them first using a blender or mortar and pestle. Then, in a small bowl, combine the flaxseeds or chia seeds with the water and soak for 10 minutes to form a gel.

3. Rinse the grated sweet potato in water until the liquid runs mostly clear. Squeeze out any remaining liquid and pat dry with a paper towel.

4. Transfer the sweet potato to a bowl. Stir in the gelled flaxseeds or chia seeds and coconut oil.

5. Shape the hash browns and place them on the baking sheet, pressing them together as best as you can. At this point, they will not hold together very well, but don't worry—they do after cooking!

6. Bake for 20–30 minutes, or until crispy and golden brown.

7. Let the hash browns cool slightly before portioning into servings for your dog. Cool completely before serving. Store any leftover portions in airtight containers in the fridge for up to 4 days.

> While both are great, white sweet potatoes are drier than the orange variety and crisp up better.

Dogranola

MAKES 750 CALORIES

You may find yourself snacking on this with your pup because it's so delicious and full of vitamin-rich seeds. The flaxseeds and chia seeds are key ingredients here: when mixed with liquid, they form a gel and bind everything together. For a lower-carb mix, simply swap the oats for more seeds such as sesame seeds or hemp hearts.

1 tbsp (8 g) flaxseeds

½ tbsp (4 g) chia seeds

¼ cup (22 g) rolled oats

⅓ cup (80 ml) water

¼ cup (30 g) raw pumpkin seeds

¼ cup (30 g) raw sunflower seeds

¼ cup (15 g) unsweetened coconut flakes

½ cup (10 g) freeze-dried fruit such as strawberries or bananas

1. Preheat the oven to 315°F (160°C). Line a rimmed baking sheet with parchment paper.

2. Lightly grind or crush the flaxseeds using a blender or mortar and pestle. Then, in a large bowl, thoroughly combine the flaxseeds, chia seeds, and oats with the water and soak for 10 minutes to form a gel.

3. Stir in the pumpkin seeds, sunflower seeds, and coconut flakes.

4. Press the seed mixture onto the prepared baking sheet into a thin slab.

5. Bake for 20–25 minutes, then very carefully flip the granola and bake for another 20–25 minutes, or until the seeds are toasty and dry. Add more time as needed, and watch closely near the end to prevent the granola from burning.

6. Let the granola cool completely on the tray. Then break it into bite-sized pieces and mix in the freeze-dried berries.

7. Feed in moderation as a treat, or sprinkled on some yogurt. Make sure your dog has enough water to drink with it. Store for up to 1 week in an airtight container in the fridge, or freeze for up to 6 months.

For smaller dogs, roughly crush or pulse the seeds in a food processor before mixing with water.

Pup English Breakfast

GRAIN-FREE 🐾 **MAKES 900 CALORIES WITH ½ CUP (125 G) SERVING OF BEANS**

A full English is truly a hearty meal. Sausages, beans, toast, eggs, bacon, mushrooms, and tomatoes* definitely make a meal fit for a dog king. Because each element is simply prepared, the flavor comes down to the quality of each ingredient. The components of our Pup English—with chicken and spinach sausages, pumpkin baked beans, and veg—are each homemade to avoid the preservatives and sugar in the conventional human versions.

This *Barked* Beans recipe makes a large batch because we use one can of beans for your convenience. You can freeze extras, turn them into a Balanced Meal (see Turkey Chili, page 69, for inspiration), or enjoy them yourself! If you like, serve this meal with a slice of Pup Bread (page 178) and/or a cup of broth "tea."

Spinach and Chicken Sausages

½ lb (227 g) ground chicken

¼ cup (25 g) finely chopped spinach

1 tbsp (15 g) tallow, butter, olive oil, or coconut oil

Barked Beans
(full batch; use ½ cup / 125 g for this recipe and save the rest)

1 (15 oz / 425 g) can unsalted navy beans, drained

1 (15 oz / 425 g) can plain pumpkin puree

¼ cup (60 ml) dog-friendly broth

Veg

1 oz (30 g) button or cremini mushrooms, quartered

2–3 cherry tomatoes, halved

1. Heat a nonstick pan over medium-high heat. Add in the mushrooms with a generous splash of water and begin cooking on medium-low heat. The mushrooms will need 15–20 minutes. (We suggest cooking mushrooms thoroughly before serving.)

2. Combine the ground chicken and spinach in a bowl. Form the mixture into sausages the right size for your pup.

3. Scoot the mushrooms to the side and add the tallow or coconut oil, then place the sausages in the pan, turning occasionally, until browned and cooked through, or internal temperature reaches 165°F (74°C).

4. Meanwhile, in a separate pot over medium heat, combine the navy beans, pumpkin puree, and broth. Stir to combine and heat until just warmed up.

5. Add the tomatoes to the pan alongside the mushrooms and sausages for just a minute to soften. Remove from heat.

6. Let everything cool before portioning into servings and plating for your dog. Store any leftovers in airtight containers in the fridge for up to 4 days.

*We avoid serving our pups large amounts of tomatoes due to the solanine in these plants (which is why we created Ketchpup), but a small serving of ripe tomatoes is just fine for dogs. Remove the stems and leaves before feeding.

Cereal Cookies

MAKES 425 CALORIES

These cookies are inspired by your favorite childhood breakfast cereals, though the flavor possibilities are endless. The base is a simple oat and coconut flour cookie. Make the cookies any color and flavor by using different dog-friendly add-ins, and cut them into any size or shape. You can't mess these up, so really set your imagination free. They're crunchy and make great gifts as well as training treats.

While you can make these with just oat flour, the coconut flour adds fiber and flavor that make them both healthier for and more appealing to your pup.

Base
⅔ cup (70 g) oat flour, plus more as needed and for rolling

⅓ cup (35 g) coconut flour

¼ cup (60 ml) water

Carob Pups
1 tbsp (8 g) carob powder

Cinnamon Pup Crunch
¼ tsp (0.5 g) Ceylon cinnamon

1 tbsp (4 g) goat milk powder

Pooch Loops
½ tbsp (4 g) each of your choice of fruit or veggie powders (beet, pumpkin, spirulina, broccoli, etc.)

Cheesy-Bones
¼ cup (50 g) shredded cheese of your choice

Other Possible Add-Ins
Ginger powder (for Gingerbark Cookies), peanut butter, or anything you can think of!

1. Preheat the oven to 350°F (175°C). Line a baking sheet with parchment paper.

2. In a medium bowl, combine the oat flour, coconut flour, water, and any chosen add-ins until you have a workable dough that is easy to roll out. If it is too sticky, add more oat flour; if it is too crumbly, add a splash more water.

3. Turn the dough out onto a floured surface and roll until it is ¼ or ⅛ inch (½ cm) thick. Use a knife or cookie cutters to cut out your desired treat shapes.

4. Transfer the cookies to the prepared baking sheet and bake 15 minutes for softer cookies or 20–25 minutes for crunchier cookies.

5. Cool completely before serving and storing. Store in an airtight container (ideally in the fridge) for up to 7 days.

DELICIOUS DOGGIE CEREAL

CINNAMON PUP CRUNCH

CAROB PUPS

CHEESY-B

DELICIOUS DOGG

POOCH

Desserts, Snacks, and Dogtails

Desserts and snacks are some of life's guilty pleasures for people, but they really needn't be. Sweets consumed after a protein-rich meal don't spike our blood sugar as much as those eaten on an empty stomach. Snacks are fine as long as we don't eat the whole bag (though we usually do). Our doggy desserts don't call for any sugar, and the dogs enjoy them all the same. If you sample any of them out of curiosity (and we suggest you do!), you might be surprised at how they taste.

Dino Nuggets

MAKES 15 NUGGETS, 700 CALORIES WITHOUT CONDIMENTS

Serve this nostalgic childhood snack to your dog after a long day at doggy day care. Don't forget a side of broccoli and one of your pup's favorite sauces, Ketchpup (page 181) or Ranch Dressing (page 201). Though the dino shapes are fun, you don't need cookie cutters to make these chicken nuggets. You can simply shape them into circles or squares with your hands.

Nuggets

1 (7 oz / 200 g) boneless, skinless chicken breast

1 egg

¼ cup (25 g) coconut flour

¼ cup (25 g) oat flour

2–4 tbsp (45 ml) water

Melted coconut oil, for greasing

Sides

½ cup (50 g) broccoli florets (optional)

Ketchpup (page 181, optional)

Ranch Dressing (page 201, optional)

1. Preheat the oven to 350°F (175°C). Line a rimmed baking sheet with parchment paper.

2. In a food processor, blend the chicken, egg, coconut flour, and oat flour, adding splashes of water as needed to help the mixture come together. The end result should be a very thick, dough-like paste.

3. Grease your hands generously with melted coconut oil. If you're using cookie cutters, grease those well, too.

4. Flatten the chicken dough into a large rectangle (about ½ inch / 1½ cm thick) on your baking sheet and cut out shapes with the greased cookie cutters. If you're not using cutters, simply form 1-inch (3-cm) balls with the dough and gently flatten them out on the baking sheet.

5. Optionally, coat a few pieces of broccoli in coconut oil and place them between the nuggets.

6. Bake for 20–25 minutes, or until the chicken is golden brown and cooked through (internal temperature should be 165°F / 75°C).

7. Let the nuggets cool completely before portioning into servings, and serve with Ketchpup and/or Ranch Dressing, if you like. Store any leftovers in the fridge for up to 4 days.

Carob Lava Cake

MAKES 2 LAVA CAKES, 450 CALORIES

This dog-friendly lava cake uses carob instead of chocolate but is just as delicious as the real thing. Trust us, we tried one (okay, several). As this recipe makes two small lava cakes, don't be afraid to eat some dog food. Just add in a teaspoon of sugar and pinch of salt to yours before baking to enjoy dessert alongside your pup.

1 large egg

¼ cup (20 g) carob powder

1 tbsp (30 g) coconut oil, melted, plus more for greasing

1 tbsp (8 g) oat flour, plus more for coating the ramekins

Fresh raspberries, for garnish (optional)

Sprig of mint, for garnish (optional)

Goat milk powder, for garnish (optional)

1. Preheat the oven to 450°F (230°C). Yes, that hot!

2. Grease two 3 oz / 90 ml ramekins generously with coconut oil. Then coat with a light layer of oat flour. This will prevent the lava cake from sticking.

3. Using a hand mixer in a mixing bowl, whisk the egg on high speed for about 3–4 minutes, or until the egg has turned pale and fluffy.

4. Gently fold in the carob powder, melted coconut oil, and oat flour until just combined.

5. Pour the batter into the prepared ramekins. Place them on a baking sheet for easy transfer in and out of the oven.

6. Bake for 4–6 minutes, or until just set and still jiggly in the middle (the jiggly centers are the lava).

7. Carefully remove the ramekins from the oven and let sit for 1 minute. Use a knife to release the edges of the cakes from the ramekins before flipping them over onto a plate.

8. Optionally, garnish with raspberries, mint, and a dusting of goat milk powder.

9. Slice into the cakes while warm to see the oozing lava and to help them cool down quickly before serving. Store any leftover portions in airtight containers in the fridge for up to 4 days.

Barkies

GRAIN-FREE 🐾 **MAKES 650 CALORIES**

We've been trying to perfect our (people) brownie recipe for years, but for some reason, the perfect brownie is always elusive. If you have any tips, please write to us. These Barkies, on the other hand, are already perfected, at least in Cedric's and Edith's eyes. Look for all-natural peanut butter made with only roasted peanuts (and no added oils, sweeteners, or salt) to make these.

1 small (8.5 oz / 240 g) sweet potato

1 large egg

¼ cup (50 g) all-natural peanut butter

¼ cup (20 g) carob powder

1. Slice the sweet potato in half lengthwise. Steam or boil until fork-tender. Let it cool slightly, then peel and mash.

2. Preheat the oven to 350°F (175°C). Grease a 6-inch (15-cm) square baking dish or line with parchment paper.

3. In a mixing bowl, whisk the egg by hand for 1–2 minutes, or just until it's light yellow and slightly fluffy.

4. Add the sweet potato and thoroughly combine with the egg. Add the peanut butter and carob powder and stir to combine.

5. Transfer the batter to the prepared baking dish. Bake for 25–30 minutes, or until set.

6. Let the brownies cool slightly before portioning into bite-sized pieces for your dog. Store any leftover portions in airtight containers in the fridge for up to 4 days.

Tip: Reserve 1 tbsp (15 g) of the whisked egg in step 3 to brush on top of the brownie before baking. This creates a subtle crackle effect like in real brownies.

Apple and Carrot Cake

MAKES 1 CAKE, 850 CALORIES

This apple and carrot cake is truly a feel-good doggy dessert. Nutrient dense with coconut oil, Greek yogurt, and hemp hearts, this treat will allow even picky eaters to enjoy their fruits and veggies.

2 large eggs

½ cup (75 g) grated apple (about ½ small apple)

½ cup (60 g) grated carrot (about 1 medium carrot)

½ cup (50 g) oat flour

Pinch of Ceylon cinnamon

3 tbsp (45 g) coconut oil, melted, plus more for greasing

½ cup (120 g) plain Greek yogurt*

1 tsp (5 g) hemp hearts (optional)

1. Preheat the oven to 350°F (175°C). Prepare a 6-inch (15-cm) square cake pan or a pan of similar dimensions by greasing with coconut oil or lining with parchment paper.

2. Using a hand mixer in a mixing bowl, whisk the eggs until they are pale yellow, frothy, and tripled in volume. This may take 3–4 minutes of whisking at high speed.

3. To the eggs, add the grated apple and carrot (save a few spoonfuls for decoration), oat flour, cinnamon, and melted coconut oil. Gently fold together with a spatula. Don't overmix.

4. Transfer the batter to the prepared cake pan.

5. Bake for 30 minutes, or until just set. Don't overbake or the cake will be too dry. Let the cake cool completely.

6. Frost with the yogurt. Top with more grated carrot and hemp hearts (if using). Serve in appropriate bite sizes, ideally with a water or a dogtail! Store any leftover portions in airtight containers in the fridge for up to 4 days.

* Got a dairy-sensitive pup? Use plain coconut yogurt instead.

All-Purpose Piecrust

MAKES 3 (4-INCH /10 CM) PIECRUSTS OR 1 (7-INCH /18 CM) PIECRUST, 650 CALORIES

Any pie is only as good as its crust. This dog-friendly piecrust ditches the wheat flour and uses oat flour (like many of our recipes). It's not that wheat flour is bad for dogs, we just prefer oat flour because it has fiber and complex carbohydrates that help control blood sugar.

3 tbsp (45 g) coconut oil, softened but not melted

1 cup (100 g) oat flour, plus more for rolling

¼ cup (60 ml) water

1. In a mixing bowl, use your hands to work the coconut oil into the oat flour, creating a grainy and coarse crumb.

2. Add the water 1 tbsp (15 ml) at a time as you knead until a workable dough forms (one that you can roll out without it being too sticky).

3. If your dough is cracking or breaking, keep adding water until it is workable with your hands.

4. On a floured surface, roll the dough out to one to three ¼-inch-thick (½ cm) slabs, depending on the size of your work surface and pie/tart pans. Then cut the dough into circles slightly larger than your pan(s).

5. Press the dough into your pie or tart pans before proceeding with a recipe.

6. You can freeze unused piecrust for 6 months or more if stored in an airtight container.

Tip: You may prebake (sometimes called blind-bake) the crust to use in your own pie or tart creation. Bake at 350°F (175°C) for 15–20 minutes, or until golden brown. Fill with your choice of ingredients.

Apple and Cheese Pie

MAKES 1 (4-INCH / 10 CM) PIE, 330 CALORIES

Apple and cheese pies have their roots in medieval Europe, where savory and sweet flavor combinations were common. Today savory and sweet pairings are just as common (think salted caramel or sweet-and-sour pork and barbecue) but are often paired with more acid. Since dogs are in pre-medieval times in terms of their cuisine, this dish is a throwback to our preindustrial roots. Plus, if your dog is picky when it comes to fruit, a little cheese wedged in there may entice them to explore this dessert!

3.5 oz (100 g) apple (about ⅓ of an apple)

1 oz (30 g) of your dog's favorite cheese

1 (4-inch / 10 cm) All-Purpose Piecrust (page 268), unbaked

1. Preheat the oven to 350°F (175°C).

2. Cut the apple in half lengthwise and remove the core. Slice the apple in half, and then slice as thinly as you carefully can with a knife. Use a mandoline for more uniform slices.

3. Slice the cheese into pieces of similar dimensions and thickness.

4. Place the cheese and apple slices in the prepared piecrust, alternating one slice of apple then one slice of cheese, until the piecrust is filled. Layering in a rosette pattern makes for a more visually appealing pie, but your dog will still like it no matter how it looks.

5. Bake for 20–25 minutes, or until golden brown.

6. Let the pie cool completely before portioning into servings for your dog. Store any leftover portions in airtight containers in the fridge for up to 4 days.

Blackberry and Beef Liver Crumble

MAKES 1 (4-INCH /10 CM) PIE, 330 CALORIES

This is another sweet and savory mixed pie to cater to dogs' refined palates. Psyllium husk is optional but helps the filling to gel.

⅓ cup (45 g) blackberries

¼ tsp (about 0.5 g) psyllium husk (optional)

4–5 small pieces freeze-dried beef liver

1 (4-inch / 10 cm) All-Purpose Piecrust (page 268), unbaked, plus leftover pastry trimmings

1. Preheat the oven to 350°F (175°C).

2. In a small bowl, mash the blackberries with the psyllium husk (if using) and beef liver.

3. Transfer the mixture to the piecrust. Use the pastry trimmings to form a crumble and sprinkle the crumbs on top of the filling.

4. Bake for 20–25 minutes, or until the filling is bubbling and the crumble is golden brown.

5. Let the pie cool completely before portioning into servings for your dog. Serve with water or a dogtail! Store any leftover portions in airtight containers in the fridge for 4 days.

When feeding psyllium husk, make sure your dog is drinking enough water. We suggest adding a splash of water into their food before serving.

Fruit Tart with Egg Custard

MAKES 1 (4-INCH /10 CM) TART, 350 CALORIES

Treat your pup to this beautiful egg custard–filled tart topped with fresh fruits. To save time, you can replace the egg custard with canned pumpkin puree or yogurt.

1 (4-inch / 10 cm)
All-Purpose Piecrust
(page 268), unbaked

1 large egg

Small handful of fruits
such as blueberries,
banana, kiwi, pineapple,
or dragon fruit

Pinch of coconut flakes
(optional)

1. Preheat the oven to 350°F (175°C).

2. Bake the empty piecrust for 20–25 minutes, until golden brown.

3. While the crust is baking, make the egg custard. Prepare a double boiler. You'll need a small pot and a heatproof bowl that fits snugly in the pot but sits high enough that it doesn't touch the bottom. Fill the pot with 1–2 inches (2.5–5 cm) of water. The water level should be just below the bottom of the top bowl. Bring the water to a gentle simmer on low heat.

4. Crack the egg into the top bowl and whisk or stir until the mixture thickens into a curd; this may take up to 10 minutes. It will get frothy first, then saucy, then thicken into the texture of a curd. If you stop stirring or the bowl gets too hot, the mixture will turn into scrambled eggs. (Your dog will still love it, but it won't look as nice.)

5. Remove the custard from the heat and let it cool slightly.

6. Transfer the mixture to your precooked piecrust.

7. Top with your dog's favorite fresh fruits and coconut flakes (if using). Optionally refrigerate the tart for 3 hours before serving to allow the curd to set.

8. Portion the pie into servings for your dog. Store any leftovers in airtight containers in the fridge for up to 3 days.

Tirawoofsu

MAKES 250 CALORIES

This Tirawoofsu, our version of the Italian classic tiramisu, will wow your dogs. (Friends and family may dig in without realizing it's not meant for them, though it is people-friendly, too!) Aside from making the Puppyfinger cookies, preparing this doggie dessert is easy. In a pinch, use store-bought dog cookies for the cookie layer. This dessert is best made with an ultra-thick, strained Greek yogurt.

3 egg whites

2 tbsp (14 g) oat flour

1 tsp (3 g) carob powder, plus more for garnish

1 cup (240 ml) warm water

1 cup (240 g) plain Greek yogurt

Puppyfingers

Puppyfingers

Puppyfingers

1. Preheat the oven to 315°F (160°C). Line a rimmed baking sheet with parchment paper.

2. In a large bowl (make sure it's squeaky-clean and dry) with a hand mixer, whip the egg whites on high speed until fluffy peaks form. This may take up to 5 minutes, so have patience. When the egg whites are thick, shiny, and opaque, they're ready.

3. With a spatula, gently fold in the oat flour until combined. Don't overmix.

4. Transfer the batter to a piping bag or use a spoon to form little log-shaped cookies, about 3–4 inches long (8 cm), on the prepared baking sheet. (Or shape the cookies to fit your chosen tiramisu dish.)

5. Bake for 15–20 minutes, or until the cookies are crispy and lightly golden. Set aside to cool.

Assemble the Tirawoofsu

1. In a bowl, stir together the carob powder and warm water.

2. Dunk each of the Puppyfingers (or biscuits if using) into the carob mixture for a few seconds on each side to wet them. Place them in a row on the bottom of a 5-inch (13-cm) square baking pan, or a similarly sized serving bowl.

3. On top of the layer of Puppyfingers, spread half of the yogurt, forming a layer about the same thickness as the cookies.

4. Place another layer of dunked Puppyfingers on top of the yogurt.

5. Add a final layer of yogurt. Dust the top with carob powder to complete the tiramisu.

6. Portion and serve immediately or refrigerate for later. Keep in an airtight container in the fridge for up to 3 days.

Soft Carob Chip Cookies

MAKES 10 SMALL COOKIES, 900 CALORIES

Chocolate chip cookies are one of those all-American desserts that are always welcome, no matter the occasion. Since chocolate usually contains theobromine, which is toxic to dogs in high amounts, we make these with carob chips instead of chocolate. These cookies come out soft. Serve with a chilled glass of goat milk for the full experience.

Carob Chips

¼ cup (50 g) coconut oil

2 tbsp (15 g) carob powder

Cookies

2 large eggs

½ cup (50 g) coconut flour

¼ cup (25 g) carob chips

Carob Chips

1. Line a 5-inch (13-cm) square baking pan (or a pan of a similar size) with plastic wrap or parchment paper.

2. Melt the coconut oil in a small pot over low heat. Remove from heat.

3. Add the carob powder to the melted coconut oil and mix well.

4. Pour the mixture into the prepared pan. Place in the freezer to cool and harden, about 30 minutes.

5. Cut the carob bar into small chunks or "chips" of your desired size. Place the carob chips in the fridge while you prepare the cookie dough.

Cookies

1. Preheat the oven to 350°F (175°C). Line a rimmed baking sheet with parchment paper.

2. In a mixing bowl, lightly beat the eggs and stir in the coconut flour until just combined. Remove the carob chips from the fridge and stir in.

3. Drop the batter by the spoonful onto the prepared baking sheet. Use a spoon or spatula to smooth the batter down into disks. Bake until just set, around 10 minutes.

4. Let the cookies cool completely before serving to your dog. Serve in appropriate bite sizes and make sure your dog has access to water. Refrigerate any leftover portions in airtight containers for up to 4 days.

Rainbow Gummies

GRAIN-FREE 🐾 **MAKES 150 SMALL GUMMIES, 125 CALORIES**

These treats are deceptive: They look just like candy but are actually high in protein and have no added sugar. You'll need silicone gummy molds, which you can easily find online. You can choose which fruit and vegetable powders you want to flavor and color your gummies. Alternatively, blend fresh fruit or veggies with the broth before heating (use ⅛–¼ cup / 20–30 g of your chosen fruit or vegetables).

3 tbsp (30 g) grass-fed-beef gelatin powder

½ cup (120 ml) cold water

1 cup (240 ml) dog-friendly broth

½ tsp (1.5 g) spinach, beet, spirulina, pumpkin, or purple potato powder

1. Put the gelatin in a large bowl with the cold water. (This allows the gelatin to soak in water and dissolve evenly, avoiding clumps. The process is often referred to as "blooming gelatin.") Set aside.

2. In a small pot over medium heat, heat the broth until it comes to a boil. Remove from the heat. Pour the hot broth into the bowl with the bloomed gelatin and stir to combine and dissolve the lumps.

3. When the broth mixture is smooth, add your choice of veggie powder and stir until well mixed. At this point, you can split the liquid into multiple small bowls to make different flavors and colors.

4. Use a dropper to transfer the liquid to your gummy molds. Refrigerate for 4 hours, or until set.

5. Pop the jellies out of the molds and transfer to an airtight container. Store in the fridge for up to 4 days or freeze for up to 6 months.

Chips

GRAIN-FREE ❧ HYPOALLERGENIC ❧ MAKES 75 CALORIES (APPLE), 40 CALORIES (ZUCCHINI), OR 200 CALORIES (SWEET POTATO) WITHOUT OPTIONAL TOPPINGS

There's something so wonderful about dogs crunching on chips, including the ASMR. These chips are the perfect healthy snack to share with your pup as you watch your favorite movie together. Though these are easy to make, they do take some time to crisp up in the oven, so make sure you have a lazy afternoon available.

1 (4 oz / 120 g) apple, 1 small (7 oz / 200 g) zucchini, or 1 small (8 oz / 240 g) sweet potato, or all three!

Optional toppings: bone broth powder, turmeric, powdered freeze-dried beef liver, or cheese powder

1. Preheat the oven to 225°F (110°C). Line 1–2 baking sheets with parchment paper.

2. If using an apple, remove and discard the apple core, stem, and seeds.

3. Slice the cored apple, zucchini, or sweet potato into thin circles. This is best done with a mandoline, as it will make extremely thin and uniform slices. You can also use a knife, but this takes patience and skill. Be careful!

4. Lay the slices out in one layer (avoid overlapping) on the baking sheets.

5. Bake for 2–3 hours, or until completely dry and crispy. If it seems like the slices still aren't getting crispy after 2–3 hours, remove the pans from the oven and let the slices sit for 5 minutes. They should crisp up when cooled; if they don't, put them back in the oven and continue dehydrating. They will get there!

6. Remove the chips from the oven and immediately sprinkle with your choice of flavors. This step is optional, but great for pickier pups.

7. Cool the chips completely before portioning and serving. Store in an airtight container for 7–14 days depending on how dry they are. A drier chip will keep longer.

Dogtail Hour

While our dog-friendly mixed drinks are fun and whimsical, there's more to them than just being props for a puppy photo shoot. Some pups dislike fruits and veggies, and one way to help with increased consumption is to mix them with a yummy liquid like bone broth. If your pup is like Edith, they prefer flavored drinks to water. These dogtails can help them stay hydrated!

Muttjito (1)

MAKES 2 SMALL MUTTJITOS, 20 CALORIES

Ingredients: 1 small sprig (3–4 leaves) mint, 4 oz (120 ml) coconut water

Garnish: 2 ribbons of thinly sliced cucumber

Wash and dry the mint leaves, then mash them using a mortar and pestle. Place the leaves, coconut water, and a few ice cubes in a cocktail shaker and shake vigorously. Pour into your cups of choice. Garnish with cucumber ribbons and serve.

Wagsky Sour (2)

MAKES 2 SMALL WAGSKY SOURS, 30 CALORIES

Ingredients: 2 oz (60 ml) dog-friendly broth, 1 tbsp (13 g) plain pumpkin puree (optional), 1 egg white

Garnish: dusting of Ceylon cinnamon

Place the broth, pumpkin puree, and egg white in a cocktail shaker and shake vigorously. (Egg whites create the layer of foam on cocktails.) Pour into your cups of choice. Garnish with a light dusting of cinnamon on top and serve.

Pup Beer/Champup (3)

MAKES 2 MEDIUM PUP BEERS OR SERVINGS OF CHAMPUP, 80 CALORIES

Ingredients: 2 tbsp (30 ml) heavy cream or 1 egg white (for the froth), 8 oz (240 ml) dog-friendly broth

Use an electric frother to whisk up the cream or egg white until it's thick and frothy. If you don't have a frother, you can shake it vigorously in a mason jar. Pour the broth into dog-safe beer mugs or cups and spoon the froth on top. Serve.

Shirley Tempup (4)

MAKES 2 SMALL SHIRLEY TEMPUPS, 20 CALORIES

Ingredients: 4 small strawberries, 4 oz (120 ml) dog-friendly broth or coconut water
Garnish: strawberry slices

Wash and dry the strawberries. In a small bowl, mash the strawberries into a pulp with a fork. Transfer the strawberries to a cocktail shaker and add the broth or coconut water. Shake vigorously. Pour into your cups of choice. Garnish each with a slice of strawberry and serve.

Pineapple Pawgarita (5)

MAKES 2 SMALL PINEAPPLE PAWGARITAS, 50 CALORIES

Ingredients: 2–3 pineapple cubes, 2 oz (60 ml) coconut water, 1–2 ice cubes (optional)
Garnish: 1 tsp (5 g) plain yogurt and 1 tsp (4 g) hemp hearts

Coat the rim of your chosen dog-safe glasses with the yogurt. Sprinkle the hemp hearts on a plate and dip the yogurt-coated rim into them. They should stick easily. Coat the entire rim of each glass. In a blender, blend the pineapple, coconut water, and optional ice cubes until smooth. Pour into the prepared glasses and serve.

Piña Coladog (6)

MAKES 2 SMALL PIÑA COLADOGS, 100 CALORIES WITH COCONUT MILK, 50 CALORIES WITH COCONUT WATER

Ingredients: ¼ banana, 2–3 frozen pineapple cubes, ¼ cup (60 ml) coconut milk or coconut water, ¼ cup (60 ml) water, as needed
Garnish: 2 pineapple cubes

In a blender, blend the banana, pineapple, and coconut milk or coconut water until smooth. Add more water as needed. Pour into your cups of choice. Garnish with pineapple and serve.

Dog Wine (7)

MAKES 1 SMALL BOTTLE OF DOG WINE, 50 CALORIES

Ingredients: handful (15 g) of berries (blueberries for Pupnot Noir and blackberries for red Bourdog), 8 oz (240 ml) dog-friendly broth

In a cocktail shaker, mash the berries to extract their juice and pigments. (Optionally, strain to remove pulp.) Add the broth and stir. Pour into a little bottle or your finest dog stemware. Serve with a Bark Wellington (page 230) dinner, of course!

Acknowledgments

This book is dedicated to all of our social media followers who guided us with their views, comments, and questions. Thank you to those who supported us from the very beginning and have even stuck around—we recognize many of you and appreciate all your kind comments and messages! Thank you to everyone who requested and then actually purchased our first PDF e-cookbook. You're why this book now exists. Even those who were highly critical served an important role in questioning the foods that we fed to our dogs. You pushed us to dig deep into the research and lean all the way in. The result is that we gained even more conviction for our mission. We are grateful for all of you.

To Stacey, thank you for believing in this book and finding the best opportunity for us to bring it to life.

To Leah, Claire, and the entire BenBella team, your diligence and expertise helped us turn our rough ideas and research into a polished book. We are grateful that we had the opportunity to work with you.

This book is the result of our best effort to reflect the state of research as of the date of submission. Despite these efforts to identify the highest-quality research, it is possible that we misinterpreted data or referenced poorly conducted studies. Any mistakes are accidental and are solely made by the authors. We apologize in advance for any oversights in judgment or interpretation.

Notes

1. Eileen K. Jenkins, Mallory T. DeChant, and Erin B. Perry, "When the Nose Doesn't Know: Canine Olfactory Function Associated with Health, Management, and Potential Links to Microbiota," *Frontiers in Veterinary Science* 5 (March 2018): 56, https://doi.org/10.3389/fvets.2018.00056.

2. Leon G. Fine and Celine E. Riera, "Sense of Smell as the Central Driver of Pavlovian Appetite Behavior in Mammals," *Frontiers in Physiology* 10 (2019): 1151, https://doi.org/10.3389/fphys.2019.01151.

3. Angela R. Brooks-Wilson, "Genetics of Healthy Aging and Longevity," *Human Genetics* 132 (2013): 1323–38, https://link.springer.com/article/10.1007/s00439-013-1342-z.

4. Mathieu Montoya, Franck Péron, Tabitha Hookey, et al., "Overweight and Obese Body Condition in ~4.9 Million Dogs and ~1.3 Million Cats Seen at Primary Practices Across the USA: Prevalences by Life Stage from Early Growth to Senior," *Preventive Veterinary Medicine* 235 (February 2025): 106398, https://doi.org/10.1016/j.prevetmed.2024.106398.

5. Judith L. Stella, Amy E. Bauer, and Candace C. Croney, "A Cross-Sectional Study to Estimate Prevalence of Periodontal Disease in a Population of Dogs (*Canis familiaris*) in Commercial Breeding Facilities in Indiana and Illinois," *PLOS One* 13, no. 1 (2018): e0191395, https://doi.org/10.1371/journal.pone.0191395.

6. Pedro H. Marchi, Thiago H. A. Vendramini, Mariana P. Perini, et al., "Obesity, Inflammation, and Cancer in Dogs: Review and Perspectives," *Frontiers in Veterinary Science* 9 (2022), https://doi.org/10.3389/fvets.2022.1004122.

7. Guido Bosch, Esther A. Hagen-Plantinga, and Wouter H. Hendriks, "Dietary Nutrient Profiles of Wild Wolves: Insights for Optimal Dog Nutrition?," *British Journal of Nutrition* 113, no. S1 (2015): S40–54, https://doi.org/10.1017/S0007114514002311.

8. Bosch, Hagen-Plantinga, and Hendriks, "Dietary Nutrient Profiles of Wild Wolves."

9. R. W. Wannemacher Jr. and John R. McCoy, "Determination of Optimal Dietary Protein Requirements of Young and Old Dogs," *Journal of Nutrition* 88, no. 1 (1966): 66–74, https://doi.org/10.1093/jn/88.1.66.

10. Eden Ephraim, Chun-Yen Cochrane, and Dennis E. Jewell, "Varying Protein Levels Influence Metabolomics and the Gut Microbiome in Healthy Adult Dogs," *Toxins* 12, no. 8 (2020): 517, https://doi.org/10.3390/toxins12080517.

11. Erin L. Streiff et al., "A Comparison of the Nutritional Adequacy of Home-Prepared and Commercial Diets for Dogs" (Waltham International Symposium: Pet Nutrition Coming of Age; Comparative Nutrition Laboratory, Texas A&M University, College Station, TX; Institute of Nutrition, University of Veterinary Medicine, Vienna, Austria; and Waltham Centre for Pet Nutrition, Leicestershire, UK).

12. Helga Gerster, "Can Adults Adequately Convert α-Linolenic Acid (18:3n-3) to Eicosapentaenoic Acid (20:5n-3) and Docosahexaenoic Acid (22:6n-3)?," *International Journal for Vitamin and Nutrition Research* 68, no. 3 (1998): 159–73, https://www.researchgate.net/publication/13646587_Can_adults_adequately_convert_-linolenic_acid_183n-3_to_eicosapentaenoic_acid_205n-3_and_docosahexaenoic_acid_226n-3.

13. Kimberly M. Heinemann and John E. Bauer, "Docosahexaenoic Acid and Neurologic Development in Animals," *Journal of the American Veterinary Medical Association* 228, no. 5 (2006): 700–705, https://doi.org/10.2460/javma.228.5.700.

14. A. P. Simopoulos, "The Importance of the Ratio of Omega-6/Omega-3 Essential Fatty Acids," *Biomedicine & Pharmacotherapy* 56, no. 8 (2002): 365–79, https://doi.org/10.1016/S0753-3322(02)00253-6.

15. Robert J. Kearns, Michael G. Hayek, John J. Turek, et al., "Effect of Age, Breed and Dietary Omega-6 (n-6): Omega-3 (n-3) Fatty Acid Ratio on Immune Function, Eicosanoid Production, and Lipid Peroxidation in Young and Aged Dogs," *Veterinary Immunology and Immunopathology* 69, nos. 2–4 (1999): 165–83, https://doi.org/10.1016/S0165-2427(99)00052-5.

16. D. W. Scott, W. H. Miller Jr., G. A. Reinhart, et al., "Effect of an Omega-3/Omega-6 Fatty Acid–Containing Commercial Lamb and Rice Diet on Pruritus in Atopic Dogs: Results of a Single-Blinded Study," *Canadian Journal of Veterinary Research* 61, no. 2 (1997): 145–53, https://www.ncbi.nlm.nih.gov/pmc/articles/PMC1189391/.

17. M. C. Ballesta, M. Mañas, F. J. Mataix, et al., "Long-Term Adaptation of Pancreatic Response by Dogs to Dietary Fats of Different Degrees of Saturation: Olive and Sunflower Oil," *British Journal of Nutrition* 64, no. 2 (1990): 487–96, https://doi.org/10.1079/BJN19900048.

18. Arnon Gal, Williams Cuttance, Nick Cave, et al., "Less Is More? Ultra-Low Carbohydrate Diet and Working Dogs' Performance," *PLOS One* 16, no. 12 (2021): e0261506, https://doi.org/10.1371/journal.pone.0261506.

19. Richard C. Hill, "The Nutritional Requirements of Exercising Dogs," *Journal of Nutrition* 128, no. 12 (1998): 2686S–90S, https://doi.org/10.1093/jn/128.12.2686S.

20. Streiff et al., "A Comparison of the Nutritional Adequacy of Home-Prepared and Commercial Diets for Dogs."

21. Patrick Nguyen, Henri Dumon, Vincent Biourge, et al., "Glycemic and Insulinemic Responses After Ingestion of Commercial Foods in Healthy Dogs: Influence of Food Composition," *Journal of Nutrition* 128, no. 12 (1998): S2654–58, https://jn.nutrition.org/article/S0022-3166(23)02281-2/fulltext.

22. S. L. Lefebvre, R. Reid-Smith, P. Boerlin, et al., "Evaluation of the Risks of Shedding Salmonellae and Other Potential Pathogens by Therapy Dogs Fed Raw Diets in Ontario and Alberta," *Zoonoses and Public Health* 55, nos. 8–10 (2008): 470–80, https://doi.org/10.1111/j.1863-2378.2008.01145.x.

23. Michael S. Leib, "Treatment of Chronic Idiopathic Large-Bowel Diarrhea in Dogs with a Highly Digestible Diet and Soluble Fiber: A Retrospective Review of 37 Cases," *Journal of Veterinary Internal Medicine* 14, no. 1 (2008): 27–32, https://doi.org/10.1111/j.1939-1676.2000.tb01495.x.

24. Harry Cridge, Sue Yee Lim, Hana Algül, et al., "New Insights into the Etiology, Risk Factors, and Pathogenesis of Pancreatitis in Dogs: Potential Impacts on Clinical Practice," *Journal of Veterinary Internal Medicine* 36, no. 3 (2022): 847–64, https://doi.org/10.1111/jvim.16437.

25. P. J. Watson, A. J. A. Roulois, T. Scase, et al., "Prevalence and Breed Distribution of Chronic Pancreatitis at Post-mortem Examination in First-Opinion Dogs," *Journal of Small Animal Practice* 48, no. 11 (2007): 609–18, https://doi.org/10.1111/j.1748-5827.2007.00448.x.

26. Mark D. Haworth, Giselle Hosgood, Katrin L. Swindells, et al., "Diagnostic Accuracy of the SNAP and Spec Canine Pancreatic Lipase Tests for Pancreatitis in Dogs Presenting with Clinical Signs of Acute Abdominal Disease," *Journal of Veterinary Emergency and Critical Care* 24, no. 2 (2014): 135–43, https://doi.org/10.1111/vec.12158.

27. O. L. Frick, "Food Allergy in Atopic Dogs," in *New Horizons in Allergy Immunotherapy*, vol. 409, *Advances in Experimental Medicine and Biology*, ed. Alec Sehon, Kent T. HayGlass, and Dietrich Kraft (Springer, 1996), 1–7.

28. I. B. Buoro, S. B. Nyamwange, D. Chai, et al., "Putative Avocado Toxicity in Two Dogs," *Onderstepoort Journal of Veterinary Research* 61, no. 1 (March 1994): 107–109.

29. N. M. Lewis, S. Seburg, and N. L. Flanagan, "Enriched Eggs as a Source of N-3 Polyunsaturated Fatty Acids for Humans," *Journal of Nutrition* 131, no. 5 (2000): 1651S–55S.

30. Cynthia A. Daley, Amber Abbott, Patrick S. Doyle, et al., "A Review of Fatty Acid Profiles and Antioxidant Content in Grass-Fed and Grain-Fed Beef," *Nutrition Journal* 9 (2010): 10, https://doi.org/10.1186/1475-2891-9-10.

31. Stefanie M. Colombo and Xenna Mazal, "Investigation of the Nutritional Composition of Different Types of Salmon Available to Canadian Consumers," *Journal of Agriculture and Food Research* 2 (December 2020): 100056, https://doi.org/10.1016/j.jafr.2020.100056.

32. Muhammad Faisal Manzoor, Tayyaba Tariq, Birjees Fatima, et al., "An Insight into Bisphenol A, Food Exposure and Its Adverse Effects on Health: A Review," *Frontiers in Nutrition* 9 (2022), https://doi.org/10.3389/fnut.2022.1047827.

33. Fiorella Lucarini, Rocco Gasco, and Davide Staedler, "Simultaneous Quantification of 16 Bisphenol Analogues in Food Matrices," *Toxics* 11, no. 8 (2023): 665, https://doi.org/10.3390/toxics11080665.

34. Xu-Liang Cao, Svetlana Popovic, and Robert W. Dabeka, "Trends of Bisphenol A Occurrence in Canned Food Products from 2008–2020," *Food Additives & Contaminants: Part A* 40, no. 6 (2023): 781–86, https://doi.org/10.1080/19440049.2023.2209898.

35. US Environmental Protection Agency, National Lakes Assessment: The Fourth Collaborative Survey of Lakes in the United States (Washington, D.C.: U.S. Environmental Protection Agency, 2022), https://nationallakesassessment.epa.gov/webreport/.

36. Kelly R. Kerr, Gary Forster, Scot E. Dowd, et al., "Effects of Dietary Cooked Navy Bean on the Fecal Microbiome of Healthy Companion Dogs," *PLOS One* 8, no. 9 (2013): e74998, https://doi.org/10.1371/journal.pone.0074998.

37. Danielle Gonin-Jmaa and David F. Senior, "The Hyperfiltration Theory: Progression of Chronic Renal Failure and the Effects of Diet in Dogs," *Journal of the American Veterinary Medical Association* 207, no. 11 (1995): 1411–15.

38. Siva Bhashyam, Pratik Parikh, Hakki Bolukoglu, et al., "Aging Is Associated with Myocardial Insulin Resistance and Mitochondrial Dysfunction," *American Journal of Physiology: Heart and Circulatory Physiology* 293, no. 5 (November 2007): H2213–22, https://doi.org/10.1152/ajpheart.00163.2007.

39. Richard C. Hill, "The Nutritional Requirements of Exercising Dogs," *Journal of Nutrition* 128, no. 12 (1998): S2686–90, https://doi.org/10.1093/jn/128.12.2686S.

40. Alexander J. German, Shelley L. Holden, Thomas Bissot, et al., "A High Protein High Fibre Diet Improves Weight Loss in Obese Dogs," *Veterinary Journal* 183, no. 3 (2010): 294–297, https://doi.org/10.1016/j.tvjl.2008.12.004.

Index

Page numbers in *italics* refer to photographs. Grain-free recipes are noted by an asterisk (*). Staple ingredients in *The Dog's Table* pantry include eggs, eggshells, eggshell powder, olive oil, oyster powder, and sea kelp powder. These ingredients are found in most recipes and are not listed separately.

About the Authors

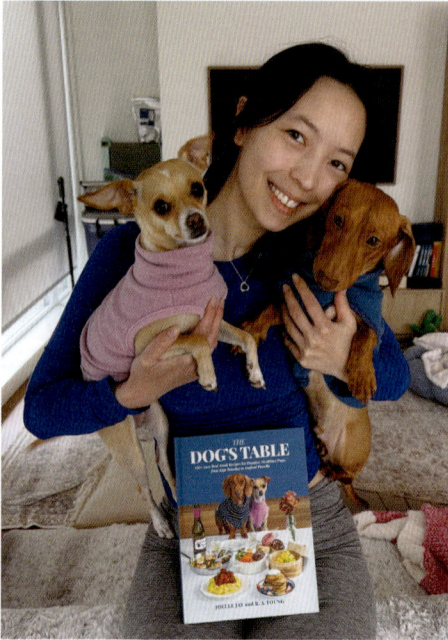

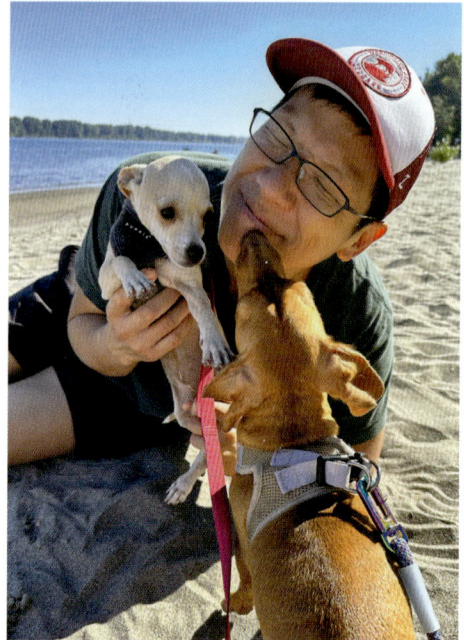

Joelle Jay is a musician, designer, and content creator. Alongside her longtime collaborator, R. A., she launched TheCedLife, a social media sensation known for creating dog meals so irresistible that even humans are jealous. In its first year, TheCedLife garnered over 200 million views. After successfully self-publishing an ebook, *The Dog's Table* marks her debut full-length print book. Joelle also serves as cofounder and creative lead of Precious Creatures Co.

Born in Hong Kong to an American father and a Chinese mother, Joelle spent her formative years between Shanghai, China, and Kansas City, Missouri, which has given her a unique cross-cultural perspective.

R. A. Young is a technologist, researcher, and content creator. As TheCedLife's audience expanded, R. A. turned his focus to the science of dog nutrition and health. He now leads the Precious Kitchen newsletter, one of the top-selling publications on Substack, and cofounded Precious Creatures Co., where he heads product development.

In addition to his work in canine health, R. A.'s expertise in AI, software, and human longevity has been featured in CNN, BBC, and the *Wall Street Journal*. Originally from Seattle, Washington, he has spent the last 20 years living across Asia, Europe, and the United States.